# Lonely Fighter

# Lonely Fighter

One Man's Battle with
the Government
of the United States

*The Story of Andrew J. Susce*

By JOHN P. HAYES

LYLE STUART Inc. · SECAUCUS, N. J.

For
Dan Mattevi
and
our ole gang

and
in memory
of Agnes Susce

First edition
Copyright © 1979 by John P. Hayes
All rights reserved. No part of this book
may be reproduced in any form except by
a newspaper or magazine reviewer who wishes
to quote brief passages in connection
with a review.

Queries regarding rights and permissions
should be addressed to Lyle Stuart Inc.
120 Enterprise Ave., Secaucus, N.J. 07094

Published by Lyle Stuart Inc. Published simultaneously
in Canada by George J. McLeod Limited
Don Mills, Ontario

Manufactured in the United States of America

Library of Congress Cataloging in Publication Data

Hayes, John Phillip, 1949–
 Lonely fighter.

 Includes index.
 1. Susce, Andrew J., 1906–   2. United
States. Internal Revenue Service—Officials and
employees—Biography.   3. Corruption (in politics)
—Pennsylvania.   4. Organized crime—Pennsylvania.
I. Title.
HJ5018.S92H39        364.1'067'09748        78-27094
ISBN 0-8184-0270-9

## Contents

Acknowledgments 7

Foreword 9

Who's Who 23

ONE  The Bureau Letter 29
TWO  The Kings 51
THREE  The Report 69
FOUR  Blowing the Whistle 85
FIVE  The Battle Begins 103
SIX  The Senator from Delaware 117
SEVEN  The Grand Jury 137
EIGHT  The Champion 151
NINE  Letters and More Letters 171
TEN  The Buck Stops Where? 197

## Acknowledgments

*Lonely Fighter* is Andrew Susce's own story. However, after more than thirty years, Mr. Susce has forgotten some of the details of his case, and so therefore I want to thank a number of individuals who helped me organize the material for this book.

Maria Zini, librarian in the Pennsylvania Division of the Carnegie Library of Pittsburgh, helped me locate material about the Mob in Western Pennsylvania. Richard McNeely, a former student of mine at Kent State University, occasionally assisted me in researching the book, as did several students in my magazine article writing classes at Temple University in Philadelphia.

Former Senator John J. Williams of Delaware was cooperative in supplying pertinent information about his investigation of the Internal Revenue Service in the early fifties. Several of the men who worked with Susce when he was fired in 1943 are still alive in Pittsburgh, but only three of them were willing to talk with me. I'm grateful for the courage of Marius Santicola, Elmer Rapp and John Orlasky. Santicola was particularly helpful when he verified Susce's account of Collector Granger's kangaroo court.

David Julyan of United States Senator Patrick J. Leahy's office supplied current information about the problems of whistleblowers, and the United States Senate Historian's office also cooperated with my requests for information about congressional matters.

Two magazine editors deserve mention for their interest in the curious case of Andrew Susce. Herb Stein at *Pittsburgh* magazine and Harry Maurer at *The Nation* both purchased my articles about Susce's battle with the Government.

Three Pittsburgh attorneys who enthusiastically contributed to the book are Malcolm Anderson, Richard L. Thornburgh and Harry Alan Sherman. These men are outstanding lawyers. Attorney Sherman, particularly, contributed tirelessly to this book, and through the years he has advised and comforted Andrew Susce.

I'm also grateful for Gwendolyn Susce, who makes the world's best lunches and knows exactly when to interrupt a long interview. And of course, I want to thank her father, Andrew Susce, a man of principle and courage.

Finally, I acknowledge my editor, Allan Wilson, my publisher, Lyle Stuart, my wife, JoAnn, and daughter, Holly, for their confidence, encouragement and understanding.

J. P. H.

## Foreword

"How would you like to write a book that will blow the lid off Washington? It involves corruption in the United States Government. It involves the Internal Revenue Service, the Civil Service Commission and . . . [there was a pause on the line before the grandfatherly voice added in a whisper] . . . it involves the Mafia, La Cosa Nostra."

At the time of this telephone call, from a person unknown to me, I was a journalism professor at Kent State University in Ohio. The era was Watergate and investigative crime stories were turning hack reporters into celebrated authors. I would have loved a crack at any one of those stories, but my newspaper days were behind me, and I had pressing matters in the classroom. Besides, I said to myself, how could anyone in Ohio know of a Government crime that would "blow the lid off Washington"?

"No," I answered flippantly into the telephone. "I value my life. I don't have any interest, but thanks for calling . . ." I tried dismissing the old man's voice as that of another nut. I had had my share of them as a reporter, and more recently as a teacher.

But the old man was persistent. "Just let me come over and talk to you," he pleaded. "I'll only take a few minutes of your time. I just want to explain this thing to you and if you're not interested, I'll go away."

More out of a wish to cut short the conversation than anything else I invited the intruder to come and tell me about his *thing*, and then I hung up the phone. "Write a book that will blow the lid off Washington," I mumbled as I walked to my classroom. "Another nut . . ."

Andrew Joseph Susce is not a nut. A bit cantankerous, yes; obnoxiously persistent, indeed. He is, nonetheless, sincere.

As we had arranged, Susce came to see me one afternoon in 1973 in Warren, Ohio. He was in his late sixties, about six feet tall and thin. As we shook hands I felt his rough, wrinkled skin and I looked into his sunken, dark eyes, circled by years of what I later learned was frustration. His head was almost pear-shaped, broad and bald above his forehead, narrowing at his chin. His cheeks were puffy and red from the winter's chill. I invited him into my cubbyhole office and he began to tell me his tale.

I knew it would take more than the "few minutes" he had requested, but after the first half hour I ignored my watch. Susce's story was not believable, but it *was* compelling, and he was a dramatic narrator. The Government of the United States, he said demurely, wanted him to commit suicide. In the mid-forties Susce had been a Zone Deputy Collector for the Internal Revenue Service and during his tenure he had investigated the Mafia boss of Southwestern Pennsylvania, John Sebastian LaRocca, alias Big John, alias the Rock. Susce claimed his superiors at the IRS had "protected" don LaRocca, who had admitted to Susce that he had bilked the Government of millions of dollars of tax money. When the IRS in Pittsburgh refused to acknowledge Susce's report and pursue LaRocca, Susce blew the whistle on his superiors. He was fired for insubordination. After thirty years, he said, the

Government continues to deny him his day in court, hoping instead that the pesky old man will die, or take his own life.

As Susce rambled, I tried interrupting him, but he wouldn't yield to me. Unlike the Government, I was a captive audience. To show my concern, I took a note now and then, particularly when Susce insisted that I remember a name or a telephone number. "Call him," he demanded of me. "Write down his name. He'll tell you that I'm telling the truth." He mentioned Richard L. Thornburgh, then United States Attorney in Pittsburgh, and Malcolm Anderson, former Assistant Attorney General of the United States.

When Susce finished his tale, I was thoroughly confused. He had recounted names of gangsters, lawyers and presidents, addresses and telephone numbers, and intricate crimes—all of which, he claimed, arose out of his investigation of John Sebastian LaRocca. The only common thread that I could detect throughout the jumbled story, however, was Andy Susce, the Government investigator, and I had my doubts about him.

"What do you want from me?" I asked Susce.

"Write a book about my case," he said. "Tell the world. You can blow the lid off . . ."

"Yes, I know," I interrupted. "But Mr. Susce, your story occurred thirty years ago and while it is dreadfully frightening, it's also very confusing. I'm sorry, but I can't help you."

The old man ignored my comment and continued his narration. "This," he said holding a legal-looking document in his outstretched hand, "will tell you all you need to know. *This* is the famous Susce Report on John Sebastian LaRocca et al." He plopped the monstrous file in my lap. "The Government didn't know it at the time, but I made a copy of this report before I turned it in, 'cause I knew it would be suppressed."

I paged through the Susce Report and started to ask a question when Susce pulled a batch of newspaper clippings out of his briefcase. The clippings were from the Pittsburgh media and they had been written about the corrupt IRS of the 1940s and 1950s. "Read through these for more information," Susce instructed me. In his next charge, he sent me to the library for a copy of the 1953 *Congressional Record* in which Senator John J. Williams of Delaware had revealed Susce's story to the United States Senate.

By this time I had decided to help the old man. He was, understandably, paranoid. He was also frightened and alone. I doubted that I could do him any good, but I pitied him, so I would try. If he had made up his story, then I might at least direct him to someone who could help him sell it as a short story or a crime novel. But if he were telling the truth—if his yarn checked out to be fact—then indeed his story ought to be told.

After contacting several of the officials Susce mentioned, including Thornburgh, I discovered that while the old man was apt to overstate, he had essentially told me the truth. What struck me most was Thornburgh's comment that "if the Susce Report had been used when it was written, it would have put organized crime out of business in Pittsburgh." That was a heady opinion coming from the United States Attorney who had taken on the Mob and won in Pittsburgh; from a man who was on his way to becoming Assistant Attorney General of the United States and several years away from a bid for the Governor's mansion in Pennsylvania. Furthermore, Thornburgh said that I could rely on Susce's memory. "He's a very conscientious person."

Susce and I began weekly meetings and even though I now believed him, I was still baffled by him. Just when I thought I understood some small segment of his complicated story, he tossed in another element and confused me all the more. At one moment he claimed that Pennsylvania's former Governor, David Leo Lawrence, had accepted protection money from the rackets, and the next moment, without expounding upon his knowledge of Lawrence, he explained how

Pittsburgh's racketeers, whom he'd listed in his report, had sold guns to Castro in Cuba. He said that Pittsburgh's late District Attorney, Robert W. Duggan, committed suicide because he had been linked to the Mob in Allegheny County, and in the next breath he charged that President Ford knew the details of his case and had promised to help, "but had done nothing."

Susce was not exactly articulate, which made his story all the more wearisome. Eventually, I told him that I couldn't help him. I had thought that I could, but it was impossible. I didn't have the time, and the old man had exhausted my sympathy.

I hadn't realized, however, that Susce was a desperate man. He was more persistent than the most determined politician. I couldn't get rid of him. He'd come to my office and spend hours showing me documents and letters, tossing out names and incidents. I'd shake my head in bewilderment hoping he'd realize that I was convinced but not interested. Instead, he ignored my unwillingness and nagged me to tell his story.

Several months after I had met Susce, I moved ninety miles from him and thought that I'd escaped him. But he was persistent. Letters, scratched out in his illegible handwriting, replaced his weekly visits. Every so often, late at night, I'd receive a phone call from him. "What's happening with my story?" he'd demand, sounding as though I were in debt to him. Finally, I decided to end our relationship. I wrote a letter to him and explained what I had been telling him verbally for so many months: "I'm not interested. Sorry. Take your story to someone else." I didn't want to offend the old man, but he had become a nuisance.

In his paranoia, Susce interpreted my letter to mean that the Mob had gotten to me. It was, he said, another "fix" in his life. In spite of that, his letters and phone calls continued.

After nearly a year, I succumbed to his tenacity, although

not entirely. I thought that I could pacify Susce by writing a magazine article about the shameful miscarriage of justice of which he had been the victim. I spent a month deciphering Susce's notes and reading his report, the contents of which had never been publicized. I contacted various sources who had been involved in the case, including Harry Alan Sherman, Susce's attorney in Pittsburgh. After several weeks of writing, I mailed the article to the first of the dozen magazine editors, who in turn rejected it. All of them responded that the article was fascinating, shocking even, but it was not "right" for their publications.

Eventually, the piece landed on the desk of Herb Stein at *Pittsburgh* magazine, and he bought it. Jubilantly, I informed Susce of the sale. I hoped the news would quiet him, but if it didn't, I was moving to Philadelphia to teach at Temple University and I felt that he certainly couldn't bother me there.

I was wrong. Within hours of *Pittsburgh* publishing his story, Susce was on the telephone. "The article is excellent, just right, but now's the time for a book," he rambled. "Things are happening. The case is hot. When are you goin' to write the book, John? You can blow the lid off Washington."

I explained to Susce that I had not changed my mind about writing a book and that my time was absorbed by other projects. Regardless of what I said, Susce pretended not to hear me, and his weekly letters continued to arrive; letter after letter after letter. Sometimes they arrived by special delivery, or by certified mail. After several months the thing became ridiculous. Many of the letters went unopened, filed instead in a thick folder marked SUSCE.

One day an idea popped into my mind that I thought would do nicely in *The Nation*. I had mailed a copy of my *Pittsburgh* article to President Jimmy Carter, feeling that his "humanitarian" administration would be responsive to Susce's case. If there was any chance of Susce's vindication, I believed Carter was that chance, and I wrote him to ask him to intervene.

Several weeks after I had mailed my article to the President, I received a letter from the United States Internal Revenue Service. The letter said, in effect, that my letter to the President had been forwarded to the Treasury Department for reply. "In the future, please refer your correspondence to file number 37600585. The case, as we've repeatedly told Mr. Susce these last thirty years, is closed."

I was outraged and disappointed. *That* was humanitarianism? How, I asked in *The Nation*, could the President of the United States serve the people when he ignored their problems?

*The Nation* piece didn't result in Susce's vindication, or even an apology from Carter, but it did attract a letter from Lyle Stuart, who asked if I was interested in turning the article into a short book. Indeed I was. At last, Susce's persistence had worn me down.

When I signed the contract to write *Lonely Fighter*, I didn't realize that Andrew Susce's story would be as relevant in 1978 as it had been in 1944. Only the players have changed in the Federal Government—the rules are practically the same. The country's three million Federal employees, who carry the weight of our national bureaucracy, are little better protected in their jobs today than was Andrew Susce thirty-five years ago. In recent years, more than one hundred Federal employees have been fired from their jobs because they "blew the whistle" on their superiors, thereby exposing inefficiency and corruption in our Government.

Consider the case of Ernie Fitzgerald, former Air Force Deputy for Management Systems. His testimony before a Congressional Subcommittee for Economy in Government exposed $2 billion of waste in the mismanagement of the Pentagon's C-5A aircraft project. After testifying, Fitzgerald returned to his office a public figure and found himself a victim of agency harassment and reprisal. Twelve days later, Fitzgerald's career tenure was revoked without explanation. Eventually he was removed from his job in a one man reduction in force. Not even the Congress could save his job!

The widely publicized Fitzgerald affair is typical of more than seventy whistleblowing cases that have been investigated by Senator Patrick J. Leahy's Committee on Governmental Affairs. In early 1978, the Vermont legislator released a report of his exhaustive study. "In recent years," he said, "increased attention has been placed on Federal employees who disclose examples of Government waste, abuse and corruption—the whistleblowers . . . they have been responsible for disclosing problems including defense cost overruns, nuclear power plant safety, conflicts of interest, and illegal or improper contracting procedures."

Senator Leahy explained that today's Federal employees are caught in a Catch-22, and "the personal risks incurred by a whistleblower make it hazardous for him to speak out." The Federal bureaucrat faces a question of allegiance. On one hand, "He is pressured by his superiors to adopt the spirit of 'team play,' placing loyalty to colleagues and agency first." On the other hand, Congress has called for a different allegiance. Federal employees are directed to place "loyalty to the highest moral principles, and to country, above loyalty to persons, party or Government Department."

This dual allegiance is an impossibility for the conscientious civil servant. And the conscientious civil servant who blows the whistle may pay a staggering price. The Government's top bureaucrats have been taught how to "properly" fire a whistleblower.

During the Nixon years, the "Malek Manual" outlined "various means at management's disposal to subvert Federal personnel law. This document described the management techniques and philosophy that can be used effectively to remove whistleblowers from their jobs," reported Senator Leahy, who along with Congressman Morris K. Udall, has introduced legislation to protect whistleblowers. The legislation, after it was watered down by the Carter Administration, became a part of the Civil Service Reform Act which went into effect in early 1979.

Here's what happens to most Federal whistleblowers:

Motivated by a personal or professional code of ethics, an employee attempts to correct a problem at the risk of his career, financial security and reputation. In the course of his efforts, the focus slowly shifts from the original problem to his own actions and conduct. Frequently, the matter becomes a procedural personnel issue. Displeased or threatened superiors are able to avoid the original issue by harassing the whistleblower. Congress and the press are often unable to render useful assistance and the courts are unwilling to interfere with what they consider an administrative, personnel matter.

The Civil Service Commission, charged with protecting employees' rights, frequently moves too slowly to provide real relief. The harassment and/or the employee's efforts to combat the harassment, triggers a grievance procedure which usually results in neutralizing the whistleblower by forcing him to concentrate on his own defense. The cost, in both financial and human terms, is overwhelming. (More than one fired Federal employee has been known to take his own life.) Eventually, the whistleblower is dismissed for insubordination, or his job is phased out of the budget.

That's what happened to Andrew Susce in 1944, when he claimed that his superiors were covering up for the Mob in Pittsburgh. The Government conveniently ignored his charges and sent a resignation for his signature. After he refused to sign, he was fired for insubordination—the Government's catch-all for whistleblowers. Almost every employee can be forced to be insubordinate.

Beyond the dangers that Susce's case spells out for Federal employees, it also serves as a warning to conscientious Americans who expect an honest Federal bureaucracy. The warning is even more urgent to Pennsylvanians, in whose state the Susce case occurred. Pennsylvanians are fearful for their state bureaucracy, as well as for their Federal agencies. By 1977, Pennsylvania had won a reputation as the nation's most corrupt state, a disreputable title that has been formerly shared by New Jersey and Maryland. Between these latter two states, however, lay a sleepy, corrupt Commonwealth that bowed to the bosses of organized crime.

In Southwestern Pennsylvania, the crime king is John Sebastian LaRocca, the man Susce investigated in the midforties. Northeast of Harrisburg, Russell Bufalino is the Mob's caporegime. Southeastern Pennsylvania is ruled by Angelo Bruno and plush Bucks County by Sam DeCavalcante. Together, these men are more powerful under the Milton Shapp Administration than the Democratic and Republican Parties combined. The Pennsylvania Crime Commission reported in 1970 that they operate more than 350 businesses in the Commonwealth. The state routinely grants business and professional licenses to these organized crime lords and awards their firms lucrative public contracts. In appreciation, the Mob pads the pockets of aspirants to the state's highest offices.

Andrew Susce had attempted to warn Pennsylvania about organized crime and the death grip in which it could hold a state government. But his report never had a chance. By the mid-forties, the Mob's power was solid in Pennsylvania's local, State and Federal agencies. It was impossible for a powerless Zone Deputy Collector to punch through the Mob's layers of protection.

Despite an influx of organized crime, Pennsylvania remained asleep through the early seventies. This phenomenon has been best explained by Wendell Rawls, Jr., who wrote in

*The New York Times* that "Pennsylvania escaped notice [because] corruption was such a way of life that there were few official complaints. The public was resigned to it, and officials thought it best to go along . . ."

The *Times'* reporter said that in Philadelphia, where Mayor Frank Rizzo had failed a lie detector examination about political deals, there was a one-hand-washes-the-other alliance between the city's Democratic machine and the Republican machine in suburban Delaware and Chester counties. The situation was similar throughout the state, and no one in Washington was much interested in action that might anger Pennsylvania's politicians.

"That's because it's an important state in national politics," continued Rawls. "For the Democrats, the high percentage of blacks and Jews in Philadelphia and Pittsburgh, combined with strong unions, makes Pennsylvania vital for a Presidential candidate. The affluent suburbs, where voter turnouts are high, are key financial strongholds for Republicans. Not only does Pennsylvania cast the third largest vote in the Electoral College (27), but its mid-spring Presidential primary often enables it to make or break a candidate, as it did Jimmy Carter, who won there in 1976, and Senator Henry M. Jackson, Democrat of Washington, who lost."

By the early seventies, Pennsylvanians had begun to challenge their corrupters. In Pittsburgh, a fiery United States Attorney by the name of Thornburgh convicted nearly forty local, State and Federal officials, including a United States Congressman. He also put away a prison full of racketeers and gangsters.

East of Pittsburgh, in the City of Brotherly Love, the clean-up was not so abrupt. There, the Special Prosecutor's Office was killed by the crooked politicians whom the office held under investigation. But by 1976 in Philadelphia, another politically hungry United States Attorney, David Marston, laid the groundwork for the convictions of the

Speaker of the State House of Representatives, the Chairman of the State Appropriations Committee, and a mouthy State Senator who had remarked of an earlier Federal prosecutor, "He can't be much of an investigator if he can't get anything on me."

Despite Marston's progress in Pennsylvania's war against organized crime, and considerable protest from citizens who wanted their state protected from criminal elements, Marston was fired in early 1978 by President Carter. The reason, said an embarrassed President, was that Marston was a Republican nominee in a Democrat's administration.

The President insisted to an unbelieving America that the ousting had not been a consequence of a telephone call from a Democratic Congressman who had asked that Marston be fired. Later, the nation discovered that the Congressman had also been a target of a Marston investigation.

The treatment of Marston in Philadelphia smacked of the Susce affair in Pittsburgh. A courageous civil servant had performed honorably for his Government, and the Government turned on him and dismissed him.

As news of Pennsylvania's war on organized crime filtered through to Andrew Susce in Ohio, he couldn't help thinking that the Keystone State would have been spared its bout with the Mob, had the United States Internal Revenue Service recognized his report in the 1940s. He was annoyed, however, when he learned that his report on John Sebastian LaRocca had been used by Richard L. Thornburgh as the background to many of the prosecutor's cases against venal civil servants and racketeers in Pittsburgh.

"Why," Susce demanded, "should the Government use the Susce Report, which I wrote, but refuse to vindicate me?" It was a question worth pursuing. Even the Ford White House had written to Susce and told him, " . . . the work you did in the 1940s proved subsequently to be very important to the Federal Government." But to this day, Andrew Susce's case is considered closed by the United States Government. Why? Why can't the Government clear his name officially? Is it because the Government fears that by honoring Susce, it will encourage other Federal employees to blow the whistle? Or is it because, as Susce says, "the Susce Report is too hot to handle in Washington. It is an embarrassment to the Democrats and it will blow the lid off Washington."

The Government of the United States owes Andrew Susce an explanation. Without one, he will never be satisfied that he was not sacrificed for being an honest agent. And the people of the United States need to be assured of their right to a responsive and efficient Federal Government.

John P. Hayes

*Philadelphia*
*November, 1978*

# Who's Who

JOSEPH D. NUNAN   Commissioner of the United States Internal Revenue Service in mid-forties. Sent to prison for tax evasion.

STANLEY GRANGER   Collector, Internal Revenue Service, Pittsburgh, 1941–1952, and Andy Susce's superior.

WILLIAM P. O'MALLEY   Deputy Collector, Internal Revenue Service, Pittsburgh, Susce's superior. O'Malley reported to Granger.

WILLIAM McCARTNEY   Another Deputy Collector, Internal Revenue Service, Pittsburgh. He also reported to Granger.

ROBERT CORY   Head of the Intelligence Division, Internal Revenue Service, Pittsburgh. He reported to Granger.

ALFRED FLEMING   Cory's boss from Philadelphia.

JOHN ORLASKY   Like Susce, he was a Zone Deputy Collector of the Bureau of Internal Revenue.

DAVID LEO LAWRENCE   Political boss of Pennsylvania in the 1940s and 1950s. Served as Mayor of Pittsburgh and later Governor of the Commonwealth. Was called "Maker of Presidents."

JAMES P. KIRK   One-time treasurer in Allegheny County and aide to David L. Lawrence. Kirk helped Susce get his job with the Bureau of Internal Revenue in 1940.

STATE SENATOR JAMES J. COYNE   Republican Party boss in Allegheny County in 1930s. Friend of the Susce family.

U.S. SENATOR EDWARD MARTIN   Former Republican Governor of Pennsylvania, served in Senate when Susce's case was revealed by Senator John J. Williams in 1953.

U.S. SENATOR JAMES H. DUFF   Former Republican Governor of Pennsylvania. Served in Senate when Susce's case was revealed by Senator John J. Williams in 1953.

JOHN S. FINE   Former Republican Governor of Pennsylvania who pardoned felony charge against John Sebastian LaRocca, thereby saving the racketeer from deportation.

CHARLES J. MARGIOTTI   Former Attorney General of Pennsylvania and attorney for John Sebastian LaRocca.

JOHN SEBASTIAN LaROCCA   Boss of organized crime in Southwestern Pennsylvania, early 1930s to date. He was the subject of Susce's tax probe.

JAMES ANGOTTI   Numbers man for the LaRocca Combine in Pittsburgh.

JOSEPH BRUSCO   Confessed racketeer, partner of LaRocca.

JOSEPH GIGLIOTTI   LaRocca partner and despised numbers collector in East Liberty.

CHARLES PAPALE   Former magistrate in East Liberty who resigned under pressure when he was suspected of protecting the rackets combine of LaRocca.

HARRY ALAN SHERMAN   Tough Pittsburgh attorney who fought the Mob and represented Susce.

U.S. SENATOR JOHN J. WILLIAMS   Broke the Susce case on the floor of the Senate, June 23, 1953.

MALCOLM ANDERSON   United States Attorney, Southwestern Pennsylvania, in the mid-fifties. Later became Assistant Attorney General of the United States.

RICHARD L. THORNBURGH   United States Attorney, Southwestern Pennsylvania, early seventies. Later became Assistant Attorney General of the United States.

E. G. TED JOHNSON   Susce's attorney in Ohio.

# Lonely Fighter

## CHAPTER ONE

# The Bureau Letter

It was April, 1943, and it was raining. Pittsburgh glistened in the morning wetness as the rain swept the city's streets and washed the soot from the brick-faced buildings. Trolleys crowded with nondescript faces sloshed along their tracks in center city while pedestrians, huddled under umbrellas, scurried to their businesses and shops. At Sixth and Grant Streets, government employees walked to their jobs in the Federal Building, headquarters for the Post Office, the FBI and the Bureau of Internal Revenue, as the IRS was then called. Among the tax agency's employees this morning was Andrew J. Susce, thirty-seven years old, and a Zone Deputy Collector.

As Susce walked to his desk on the fourth floor, he chatted aimlessly with John Orlasky, a fellow employee. They exchanged complaints about the seemingly unending rains. Susce suggested, not so facetiously, that Pittsburgh could be swallowed by a flood, not unlike the one that had whipped through the city in the spring of 1936, killing seventy-four persons and leaving behind nearly $100 million in property damage. It was a frightening thought, dismissed as quickly as it had been uttered.

On the fourth floor, Susce walked to his mail slot, or pigeon hole, as they called it in the Federal Building. Most mornings, Susce's pigeon hole was empty, save for a note from his superior or a late payment from a taxpayer in one of his wards. Nonetheless, efficiency dictated Susce's checking the slot every morning, first thing, and then once again before leaving the office for the day. This morning, to Susce's surprise, he found a government envelope in his pigeon hole addressed to: Mr. Andrew J. Susce, Twenty-third District, Pittsburgh, Pa. Sensing its urgency, Susce ripped open the envelope. Certainly it wasn't a raise; it wasn't that time of year. A promotion? Not likely. He'd been told he was being considered for the Intelligence Division, but he didn't expect that news until the fall.

As he removed the letter from the envelope and unfolded it, he noticed that it had been signed by William P. O'Malley, Deputy Collector of the tax bureau in Pittsburgh. He knew then that it couldn't be a promotion. Those letters were signed by Stanley Granger, Collector of the local bureau and the top tax man in Pittsburgh. O'Malley's letter, it turned out, was simply a formality, directing the Zone Deputy Collector's attention to an attached letter from J. Edgar Hoover, Director of the Federal Bureau of Investigation. Now oblivious of several of his co-workers who had gathered around their mail slots for a chat, Susce carefully read Hoover's letter. It was only a paragraph but Susce read it slowly, and then he read it a second time, uncertain of what to make of it. Hoover had written to Joseph D. Nunan, Commissioner of the Bureau of Internal Revenue, Washington, D.C., requesting an investigation of the tax records of John Sebastian LaRocca, a resident of Pittsburgh. The FBI's chief executive officer said he had reason to believe that LaRocca was evading his taxes and he also suspected that LaRocca was operating a numbers racket. The latter being more difficult to prove than the former, Hoover asked that the Bureau of Internal Revenue conduct an investigation.

For a moment, Susce stood motionless, numbed by the impact of his mail. Hoover's request was known among taxmen as a "bureau letter" and it commanded priority attention. Upon receipt of a bureau letter, work in progress had to be dropped and the assignment carried out at once. In the three years that Susce had been with the tax agency, he had received two prior bureau letters, so he was aware of the implications. However, neither of those letters had been personally signed by J. Edgar Hoover. Nor had they accused a racketeer. This morning's letter was not a routine check of just any taxpayer's records. This letter asked for an investigation of the business of John Sebastian LaRocca, destined to become the boss of organized crime in Southwestern Pennsylvania. Such an investigation, successfully conducted, would be political suicide, Susce knew. Pittsburgh's racketeers were protected in high places. Susce had a family to support and a career to nurture. He couldn't possibly accept Hoover's bureau letter. This was not a job for a Zone Deputy Collector, a man least protected among employees of the Federal Government. This belonged to the Intelligence Division, Susce thought. Those boys would know how to handle John LaRocca. They had put away Al Capone in the thirties. They should be given a crack at Pittsburgh's Big John, the Rock.

"Andy, you dreamin'?"

Susce looked up from his mail and into the face of Orlasky, whom he had greeted earlier in the morning. "John," he said solemnly, "look here what I got. J. Edgar Hoover wants me to investigate John Sebastian LaRocca."

"What?" Orlasky exclaimed, looking astonished. "You can't do that, Andy. Do you know who he is?"

"Of course I know. And I'm not gonna do it."

Before Orlasky could ask Susce how he planned to get out of the assignment, Susce was headed for O'Malley's office.

"Bill," Susce said as he stood in the Deputy Collector's office. "Look here what you gave me."

Already buried in his morning paper work, O'Malley took the letter from Susce's hand, knowing, of course, what it was about.

"I can't do this, Bill. This is for someone else."

O'Malley removed his glasses and examined the bureau letter. Without lifting his head the Deputy Collector peered up at Susce. "You don't want it, Andy?"

"Naaaa, give it to Intelligence. Those fellas can handle it."

"All right, Andy, I'll see what I can do." O'Malley's eyes returned to the papers on his desk and Susce left the office.

Believing that he'd been released from Hoover's investigation, Susce felt relieved and returned to his desk to begin his routine assignments. The bulk of the season's tax load had passed,* but Susce was catching up with taxpayers who were delinquent, or confused by the Government's intricate tax forms. Basically, Susce's job consisted of simple mathematics, but he thrived on it. Every day was different. New problems, new faces. Half of his time was spent "in the field" where he assisted shut-ins and small businessmen who had trouble figuring their taxes.

Most of all, Susce loved the respect that was afforded an agent of the Federal Government. To Susce, there was no greater honor, after serving God, than serving the United States Government. It was a dream come true for this son of Slovakian (later Czechoslovakia) immigrants who had been attracted to Pittsburgh's flourishing steel industry in the late eighteen hundreds.

---

*In those days, the deadline for filing income-tax returns was March 15.

Paul Susce was sixteen when he realized the opportunities that existed in America. He was one of four children whose father was a caretaker of a baron's estate. Poor, and without promise of a better life, Paul decided to emigrate. One night, disturbed about leaving home and afraid he wouldn't go if he didn't go immediately, Paul slipped into his parents' bedroom, kissed his mother and father while they slept, and slipped away. He arrived at Ellis Island sometime in 1890 and from there went to live with relatives in Mount Washington, Pa. Later, he moved to Braddock, Pa., the melting pot for Slavs who had been drawn to the Pittsburgh area. Ninety percent of Braddock was Slavic and sooner or later, most Czechs who immigrated to Pittsburgh moved to Braddock. In time, Paul was joined by one of his brothers and his two sisters. A second brother, Michael, remained in his native land with his parents and, oddly enough, became a millionaire.

In 1900, Paul met and married Mary Yager. Her parents were farmers in Slovakia and while they were not poor they nonethless encouraged Mary and one of her sisters to go to America for the chance of a better life. Mary was about twenty when she married Paul Susce in St. Elizabeth's Church in Pittsburgh. The couple settled at Hodge Street, Number Eight, on Calico Hill, which was within walking distance of the Jones and Laughlin Steel Company where Paul was employed. He remained in the mill until he retired during the Depression.

Predominantly Irish, Calico Hill was so named because on feast days of the Catholic Church the Irish dressed in robes of calico.

As the Susces established themselves on Calico Hill they came to be regarded as people of principle and character. Bad times had driven them from their homeland but could not deprive them of generations of tradition and devoutness. While they had adapted to their new country, their habits still reflected their old way of life. On Sundays they worshiped in the mornings, relaxed after a plentiful home-cooked dinner, and then later returned to church for evening vespers. Through the week, Mary remained at home, baking, cleaning, caring for the house. In every room she had hung a religious painting, or a crucifix. Her home was as much a temple for the Lord as it was a shelter for her and her husband. Of course, it was also open to her neighbors, whose mid-morning visits were given zest by gossip and strong coffee.

Paul, meanwhile, earned his wage of one dollar per day at the steel mill. Paul Susce was a gentle man, recognized for his dependability and sincerity. He was well liked by his neighbors as well as by his employer.

Like most couples on Calico Hill, the Susces were happy. They weren't poor, at least not by their standards, but they knew little about affluence. That didn't matter. They didn't own a car so they rarely traveled beyond their district. They walked to the store, to the church, to the mill. Their social life included a stroll in the park or maybe a movie, but most of their leisure was spent visiting their neighbors and friends. Above all, the Susces lived as honest, loyal Americans and became exemplary models for their children.

Within ten years, four sons were born to the Susces. John was their first. He was followed on January 20, 1906, by twins, Michael and Andrew. A few years later, George was born.

One of the fascinations of childhood in Andrew Susce's time was the lamplighter. Every evening around five o'clock in the winter, later in the summer and spring, the lamplighter walked the streets of Calico Hill and lit the gas lamps. Early every morning he returned to put out the lights. Andy and his brothers often trailed behind him as he made his evening rounds.

When the circus came to Oakland, which was north of Calico Hill, Paul Susce took his boys to the show and afterwards treated them to ice cream cones. On Sunday afternoons, Paul often took the boys for a walk through the park. In the summer they went swimming and fishing and in the winter, sledding and ice skating.

Andy Susce enjoyed a typical childhood, one that could be expected of a boy with respectable, God-fearing parents. It was a childhood of the kind of humble culture which was built around family unity and service to God and country and mankind. This was a creed of sorts for the Susces.

A young woman who lived next door to the Susces in Calico Hill escorted Andy to his first day at Holmes School in Pittsburgh. He spent four years at Holmes and earned credit for five years of schooling. He was promoted from the second to the fourth grade, without ever attending third grade. By the sixth grade, Andy was enrolled in St. Joachim's Catholic school, where he was taught by nuns and priests. Holmes School was educationally sound, but Andy's parents favored sending him where his religious beliefs, so thoroughly drilled into him at home, could be reinforced. While he was at St. Joachim's, Andy sang in the choir and served as an altar boy.

Academically, Andy was better than average in several subjects. He excelled in mathematics, religion and science. He impressed his peers and teachers with the questions he sometimes asked. Once, however, it was discovered that Andy was reading St. Thomas Aquinas' *Summa Theologica*. The discovery disturbed the nuns who were afraid that the book was too deep for a fourteen-year-old. They sent Andrew for a chat with the parish priest who suggested that the young man refrain from reading the writings of St. Thomas. Andy explained that he intended to make the priesthood his vocation and he was trying to prepare himself for that future. Just the same, the priest advised, he was too young for such deep thinking;

clearly not the first, or the last, parish priest thus to express fear of the great mystics of the church.

If any subject was a problem for Andy, it was English. The language was foreign to the young man. Not that he didn't try. He read books tirelessly. But English, which was not spoken well in his home or among his neighbors, would be an embarrassment to him throughout his life. Nonetheless, an aggressive young Susce persevered and made himself understood.

After his graduation from St. Joachim's, Andy was enrolled in Duquesne University Prep School in 1921. That same year his parents bought a home at 14 Ayres Street, Calico Hill, overlooking the area which was later developed into Pittsburgh's Parkway East. It was about a thirty-minute walk from his parents' home to the all-boys prep school, but the education and opportunity were good. Besides, friends accompanied him to school: Mike Dudick, a neighbor, became a doctor; Paul Jennings, another neighbor, became a city administrator in Pittsburgh. Duquesne's Prep School was not tuition-free, but with his father's help and summer income from working as a grocery delivery boy and later in the steel mill, Andy paid his way.

The Holy Ghost Fathers were the administrators and teachers at Duquesne and they insisted upon discipline and high academic standards. It was a rule that students wear ties to class. Tardiness, of course, was a major offense and violators were severely reprimanded. Students were not free to select their own subjects of study; instead they were told what courses to take. All students were tested quarterly by written and oral examinations.

Andy Susce was an honor student in many subjects, including Greek, history, Latin and mathematics. He particularly liked history and theology. Throughout prep school, Susce thought of the priesthood as his vocation and he received encouragement from the Holy Ghost Fathers.

However, by the time he graduated from Duquesne, in 1925, Susce had changed his mind about the priesthood. He decided, instead, that he'd study to become a doctor and he enrolled in a pre-med program at Duquesne University.

College was out of the reach of Paul Susce's limited income, but the fact that his son had the opportunity to go beyond a secondary education was proof that the immigrant's belief in the American dream was not in vain. Opportunity for all was indeed a possibility. To help his son, Paul Susce, by this time a foreman at Jones and Laughlin, arranged for Andy to be hired full-time in the mill. Young Susce worked days and attended school part-time in the evenings. And that's how it happened for four years, with Susce paying for school himself and living with his parents and brothers on Calico Hill. It was a slow education and Susce often felt he was making little progress, but he persevered. He wanted desperately to become a doctor.

By late 1929, however, his plans were spoiled. In the late twenties, there were hints of depression in various segments of America's economy, including the automotive industry which was dominated by Henry Ford. Layoffs were common and unemployment increased though sometimes softened by a shorter work week and fewer working hours per day. Early in 1929, Herbert Hoover was inaugurated President of the United States and the economy looked healthy and prosperous. But by December of that year, the stock market collapsed, and so did the expectations of Susce and millions of his fellow Americans.

One of the first men to be let go from Jones and Laughlin Steel Company was Andy Susce. And not long after him, Paul Susce was forced into early retirement on $49.80 a month. Fortunately, Paul and Mary Susce had been thrifty. They had not lived their lives foolishly and they had saved money during the good years. They weathered the Depression. But Paul realized that his pittance of a pension, even when coupled with his savings, would hardly support his unemployed family. Fortunately, James J. Coyne, the Republican State Senator of the forty-fifth district, where the Susces lived, was a friend of the family. He arranged for Paul to be hired as the caretaker of the nearby park system and the income from the job sufficiently supplemented the Susces' livelihood so that the family could survive.

Andy Susce did not find full-time work again until the summer of 1930. He contributed to his family's welfare by working occasional odd jobs, as did his brothers, but permanent work was not available. Unemployment became his way of life. But millions of Americans suffered with him.

Oddly 1930 was a significant year for Andy Susce, despite the hardship it brought him. Three events of that year were, for him, memorable. They were, in this order, his marriage, a full-time job, and the birth of his first child.

It was on a Sunday in late 1929 on Calico Hill when the Susces were visited by distant relatives from Wheeling, W. Va., and Andy met his striking fourth cousin, Agnes Lendak. Young Susce fell in love with her and he and Agnes were married on his birthday, January 20, 1930. He was twenty-four years old and his bride was eighteen. The wedding ceremony was performed in St. Joachim's before a gathering of friends that included several of the nuns and priests who had encouraged Andy Susce to enter the seminary.

Marriage in 1930 was courageous by anyone's standards. It was, perhaps, an escape from the doldrums of the Depression but it was also daring in the case of two people without jobs or other financial security. But Andy Susce was not a patient man and he wasn't about to give Agnes Lendak a chance to escape him. He had never seen, he thought, a more beautiful woman, and one with so much spunk. Besides, he explained to his parents, if he had to live an impoverished life, he should at least have the comfort of a loving wife.

Despite an already difficult situation, the newlyweds moved in with Andy's parents, who didn't seem to mind.

Now, of course, Andy spent his days looking for a permanent job. About six months after the wedding, he was in downtown Pittsburgh one afternoon when he met the family friend, Senator Coyne. The honorable politician was walking up Grant Street, enroute to the courthouse, when Susce recognized him and approached him with hand outstretched. He was warmly received.

"Andrew, my boy, how's the family?"

"Not well, Senator. We're broke. Flat as a pancake."

"We all are, son, we all are," replied the politician. "How's your wife?"

"Fine, Senator," Susce replied.

"Are you working?"

"Not since the steel mill, sir. Do you know of any work?" Susce asked, his eyebrows raised in hopeful anticipation.

"I'll let you know if I do, son. Say hello to your daddy for me. Gotta go."

Susce's spirits weren't raised much by the Senator's remarks but about ten days later he received a letter requesting him to report to the Department of Highways. He did so immediately and when he showed his letter to the clerk on duty he was asked, bluntly, "What kind of job do you want?"

Flabbergasted, Susce took a step backwards. He had no idea it would be so easy. "What kind of job can you give me?" was the best answer he could manage.

"Can you drive a truck?"

"Nope, never learned to drive." It was true. Susce had never sat behind the wheel of an automobile. His family was too poor to own one, so what sense was there in learning to drive? "I can keep books, though." If possible, Susce preferred a job that would make use of his education, but he wouldn't be obstinate.

"You're going to work," said the clerk. "You can be a timekeeper. Report here tomorrow morning."

Susce didn't know what the job entailed or what it paid but he didn't care. He darted home and told his wife and parents the good news. At last, a full-time job. As timekeeper, Susce kept track of the man-hours spent on road repairs in Allegheny County and in effect was the bookkeeper for various construction projects.

The job was not only well suited to his capabilities, but well timed. Agnes was pregnant. Shortly after his first day on the job, Susce rented an apartment in Wexford, not far from his parents' home and conveniently located for his work.

That November, a daughter was born to Agnes and Andy Susce and they named her Gwendolyn.

Marriage, a job and then a child—and all of it in the midst of a depression. Andrew Susce was lucky. Thousands of unemployed men had met violence in the streets of America's major cities while demonstrating for better lives in 1930. Thousands of others had sat, drowning in poverty and bad luck, full of self-pity. But Andrew Susce had weathered the storm.

Two years later, however, Susce was again unemployed but this time it was by choice. For some unknown reason, perhaps political, a superintendent approached Susce one morning and informed him that he was no longer a timekeeper.

"Why?" Susce demanded to know.

The explanation was mumbled but Susce understood that the superintendent wanted to give the timekeeper's job to another man, a friend of his, and Susce was being sent to the construction crew.

"No, sir," Susce protested, "I'm not a laborer. I was hired to be a timekeeper. You can take me home before you can make me labor."

Without arguing, the superintendent arranged for Susce to

be driven home, since the work site that day was several miles from Wexford. When Andy entered the front door of his apartment, Agnes wondered if he had been injured.

"What are you doin' home, Andy?"

"I quit. I'm not a laborer. They want me to go on the crew so I quit." Susce half mumbled his answer as he searched for Senator Coyne's telephone number. He wanted an explanation. The Senator, however, was surprised to hear of Susce's situation and told his friend that he'd handle the matter. Sure enough, the next Monday at eleven o'clock in the morning, Charles King, of the Department of Highways, drove to Susce's apartment in a car owned by the State of Pennsylvania.

"I was told to drive out and pick you up for work," King told Susce at his front door. "We need a timekeeper."

"Be with you in a minute," Susce said smugly. "Come in while my wife packs me a lunch."

Back on the job, Susce met the superintendent and explained that he wouldn't have minded working as a crewman but he was hired to be a timekeeper. "Principles come first in my book," he told the still stunned superintendent.

Six months later Susce was booted out of his timekeeper's job a second time, but he was promoted to foreman. Along with the promotion came a pay increase so that he earned more than $125 a month.

By 1936, Susce had tired of the foreman's job and when he wasn't promoted to a better position he resigned. He had saved some money, and even though he now had a son, Andrew, Jr., to care for in addition to his wife and daughter, he wasn't financially pressed. Apart from this, his mother had died in 1932 and his father was at home alone where he needed someone to care for him. Susce's apartment was too small for his father to move in, so he moved Agnes and the children to Calico Hill.

Not long thereafter, Susce was hired by the City Streets

Department under the federally financed Works Progress Administration. The job paid $15 a week. Six months later, that job petered out and Susce was hired as a foreman by the City Streets Department where he earned about $25 a week. He worked as foreman through 1940 when a friend told him that James P. Kirk, county chairman of the Democratic Party and a city treasurer, was looking for men to work for him.

During the Depression, Susce had decided that political contacts would be to his advantage. Republican Senator Coyne was proof of the theory. Not only had he helped Andy's father, but he had also assisted Andy on more than one occasion. The "Hoover Depression," however, had caused a blight upon the Republicans and even though Andy's father had been a loyal GOP supporter all his life, Andy had changed his own political affiliation by 1932, when Franklin Delano Roosevelt buried incumbent President Hoover and his followers in the election of 1932.

Susce had enthusiastically supported Roosevelt; even attended a political rally in Harrisburg at the invitation of Eleanor Roosevelt, the President's wife. Susce's loyalty wasn't unnoticed by Jimmy Kirk. Susce had himself made certain of that. He knew that Jimmy Kirk was a powerful voice in Pittsburgh's political arena as the right-hand man of David Leo Lawrence, the physically rugged, athletic politico who served as Pennsylvania's Democratic National Committeeman. Lawrence, oddly enough, was a business partner of GOP Senator James J. Coyne in the Coyne-Lawrence Insurance Agency.

Susce visited Kirk one afternoon and asked him for a job. Kirk remembered Susce and hired him as an assistant in the City Treasurer's office. Several months later, when Susce heard there were openings in the Bureau of Internal Revenue, he asked Kirk to get him a job with the agency. Again, Kirk happily intervened for his friend Susce and after

Susce was interviewed by the local Bureau of Internal Revenue, he was notified to report for work.

One of the most important moments in Susce's life occurred in December, 1940, when he was sworn in by the dignified William Driscoll, Collector of the Bureau of Internal Revenue in Pittsburgh. To work for the United States Government—not only the Government, but for President Franklin Delano Roosevelt, the great liberator—it was without doubt the greatest honor ever bestowed upon Andrew J. Susce. The appointment ended any lingering sadness that he felt about not becoming a doctor. In his family and neighborhood of Calico Hill, he was now a man of importance, a hero of sorts who deserved the respect of every citizen. The Bureau of Internal Revenue was, after all, responsible for law and order, for putting away men like Al Capone, the Chicago gangster.

The Bureau of Internal Revenue was American. And its agents were men of scrupulous reputations. To be counted among them was as honorable as serving in the Federal Bureau of Investigation or the Senate of the United States. And Andrew Susce did not, even for a moment, allow himself to believe otherwise. There was nothing improper, of course, about being a political appointee. Most of the men who worked with Susce had won their jobs through politicians. That, he had learned, was the American way. It was the system; Andrew Susce had played fairly and won.

As a Zone Deputy Collector, Susce earned about $150 a month. His job description read (in part): (1) Makes special field investigations of the various tax cases in unusual and complex types which require especial demonstrated ability for investigational work . . . (2) . . . serves warrants for distraint to collect taxes due and unpaid . . . (3) . . . assists taxpayers in the filing of tax returns; and (4) performs related or similar tasks of a comparable degree of difficulty as assigned.

In the 1930s and 1940s, the Bureau of Internal Revenue included a much greater proportion of political hacks than it would in later years. At the head of the local office in Pittsburgh, as was the case in other branch offices throughout the country, was the Collector. The position was a political plum, as were most of the positions of authority within the agency. William Driscoll was the Collector at the time Susce was hired but he retired not long thereafter and Stanley Granger was appointed to succeed him. A former United States attorney, Granger resembled The Great Gildersleeve of television comedy. He was an appointee of the political machine of David L. Lawrence and as such was a political puppet whose main interest seemed to be to please Lawrence and the local politicos. Granger developed a reputation for incompetence but his greatest asset was that he was loyal to the politicians who kept him in office.

Reporting to Granger were several Deputy Collectors, including William P. O'Malley, an appointee of United States Senator Joseph Guffey, Lawrence's political foe. O'Malley was a few years Granger's senior and he despised the boss for his ineptness. Moreover, O'Malley had expected to be appointed Collector before Granger, but the weak arm of Senator Guffey had fallen to the strong arm of Davey Lawrence. Regardless of O'Malley's personal feelings, however, he was attentive to Granger's directives. After all, the Deputy Collector had a family who depended on his job.

Another Deputy Collector was William McCartney, a Lawrence loyalist who kept company with Pittsburgh's known racketeers. McCartney developed the reputation of hatchet man in the local bureau. Bigoted, he thought the only good man was an Irishman and he scorned men of any other nationality.

These were the top men who supervised some three hundred federal tax employees in the Pittsburgh office of Internal Revenue. Had Andy Susce been privy to the politics of the Pittsburgh tax office, he might have felt differently about joining the force. At least he mightn't have been so jubilant following his induction.

Furthermore, had the taxpayers of Calico Hill understood the political influence in their local tax office, they would have considered Andy Susce somewhat less of a hero and more of a political opportunist. But few people suspected politicians in the Roosevelt era. The immediate problems created by the Depression and later by World War II diverted the thoughts of Americans from the affairs of politicians.

During the first few months of Susce's employment he was teamed up with John Orlasky, a veteran Zone Deputy Collector who was recognized for his conscientious work. He, too, was a political appointee. The idea was for Orlasky to teach the job of Zone Deputy Collector to Susce. Collector Driscoll also taught Susce how to complete various tax forms and he helped him interpret pertinent tax laws. To sharpen his skills, Susce enrolled in accounting courses at Duquesne University. He intended to make the Bureau of Internal Revenue his career. If he could, he'd go to the top, maybe seek a job in the Washington office, or perhaps the Intelligence Division.

Susce was a fast learner. Figuring taxes and filling in forms were a task that he mastered in the first few weeks on the job. Almost as quickly, he became familiar with the statutes that Zone Deputy Collectors were expected to know as they worked "in the field" or in their wards. At home, Susce memorized the statutes and practiced them before his wife and friends.

Eventually, and unfortunately, Susce was assigned the eleventh, twelfth and thirteenth wards of the City of Pittsburgh. What Susce didn't know was that these wards, which included commercial East Liberty in northeast

Pittsburgh, were infested with racketeers of the worst sort. The area was a fifteen minute drive by car from center city Pittsburgh.

Susce, of course, because he didn't drive, either walked his routes or rode on public transportation. His clientele consisted primarily of blue collar families, some of whom had political influence, but most of whom had little interest in politics. There were millmen, factory workers, shop owners and other businessmen, the wealthy as well as the poor. All of them were supposed to pay taxes and Andrew Susce made certain that they did. Of course, it wasn't within his authority to pick someone at random and investigate his tax records. Susce didn't go looking for tax violators. Instead, he checked out complaints that were filed against taxpayers in his wards or he validated returns that were rejected by suspicious eyes.

Businessmen, on the other hand, were not so immune from tax investigation. Once every year Susce had the right to check a businessman's returns, including his Social Security forms. One of Susce's duties was to collect a special tax levied on juke boxes, pinball machines and one-arm bandits. Twenty dollars annually was the tax on each machine and the owner had to display a license in the event the tax man came inspecting. Susce's wards were filled with taverns, amusement centers, cigar stores and haberdasheries—all prime spots for one-arm bandits.

In August, after the special tax was due, Susce visited every likely spot in his wards, checking licenses and collecting taxes from delinquent owners. It wasn't uncommon for Susce to enter a tavern and find five or six unlicensed machines. On the spot, he'd figure the tax due, collect it and press the owner for any other machines that he owned in the wards. Susce didn't ask the owner if he knew of others who were delinquent, for that question wasn't ethical, but it wasn't unusual for an owner to squeal on one of his "friends." Equal taxation, after all, was never intended for a select few.

Some days, in the field, Susce collected thousands of delinquent tax dollars in cash, always cash, for the government refused checks or money orders as payment for the special tax.

About half of Susce's job was devoted to collecting delinquent federal taxes and the other half consisted of paper work and investigations. During the tax season, which ran from the first of the year until March 15, the filing date, Susce worked at the federal building where he, and most other Zone Deputy Collectors, assisted anyone who came looking for help in calculating his taxes. In Susce's time, nearly fifty percent of all taxpayers went to the Government with their tax problems and forms, and not to private tax assessors. During the war, Susce was even sent to factories where he assisted workmen who were caught up in the war effort.

Most of Susce's clients in the field were of Italian descent. Like the Irish and Slavs of Calico Hill, the Italians respected an agent of the United States Government. They cooperated with the tax man willingly. They knew, by his sincerity and enthusiasm, that Susce was an honest man. Susce acquired a reputation for knowing the business of his wards, and the businessmen who operated in his area recognized Susce's skill and authority. Occasionally, some tavern owner would hassle Susce about all the taxes he had to pay, but Susce was never threatened or harmed. He encountered few problems collecting delinquent taxes and he always met the monthly quotas that were established by the bureau to measure his productivity.

By April of 1943, when Susce received the bureau letter concerning the investigation of John Sebastian LaRocca, he had received several routine pay increases and "satisfactory" merit ratings for his work. There were no complaints about his productivity, which usually exceeded most other field agents in the bureau's employ. He was considered an asset to the government and a loyal civil servant. Conversely, Susce had few complaints about his job, though he was curious about some of the business that went on above him. Nonetheless, his morale was high and he never lost the enthusiasm that he had brought to the position. The Bureau of Internal Revenue was his oasis in a desert of financial insecurity. Susce wanted to protect it. He knew, of course, that an investigation of John Sebastian LaRocca could turn his oasis back to desert. The problem was to shake himself loose of it.

"Andy," O'Malley said after summoning the field agent to his office, "Granger says you have to take this case. You're the man for it. LaRocca lives in your area."

"But what about Intelligence? What about Cory?" (Robert Cory was Chief of the Intelligence Division.)

"Granger says you're the man, Andy. I'm just following orders," O'Malley said curtly. By the tone of his voice, Susce knew that the Deputy Collector also believed the LaRocca investigation belonged to Cory's division.

"Bill, there are going to be problems with this report. You know who LaRocca is. I don't know where it'll stop. Do you want a whitewash?" Susce figured a whitewash was his best chance for survival.

"Andy, I don't give a damn where it leads. No matter how long it takes I want you to conduct a complete investigation and let the chips fall where they may, no matter who it hurts." O'Malley knew, better that Susce, that an investigation of John Sebastian LaRocca would lead to one central figure: David Leo Lawrence. And Senator Guffey would be proud of his boy Bill.

"What protection do I have, Bill?" Susce was searching for another way out. He knew as well as anyone in the bureau that a political appointee had no protection. He could be hired one moment and fired the next at the whim of his superior, Stanley Granger.

"Do your duty, Andy. The power of the United States

Government is behind you. No matter where it leads, the Government will back you up. You want to get into Intelligence? This will be good training. Good luck."

Susce left the Federal Building that afternoon in a downpour of rain. He was going home to give thought to his dilemma. He knew he could resign, but for the first time in his life he felt he had a future working for the bureau. And he needed the job. There was always the possibility of turning in a whitewash. To hell with the power of the United States Government, he thought. Bill O'Malley was looking out for Bill O'Malley; that much Susce knew about politics. But a whitewash would be dishonest. Principles had always come first in the Susce family. Honesty was a creed. Susce searched for a proper answer among the pounding raindrops, but there was none.

CHAPTER TWO

# The Kings

By the time Andrew J. Susce had been hired by the Bureau of Internal Revenue in 1940, the Mafia was already dead in America. The secret society, in fact, had spread its menacing tentacles into many sensitive areas of American life and died suddenly before the word Mafia was created. It was, however, a death of convenience. When the society died, its evil tentacles were not withdrawn. Rather, they remained to be nurtured by sophisticated, white-collar criminals who used lower class thugs to capitalize on the country's economic and social weaknesses. By the mid-1930s, the National Crime Syndicate—the Mob, the Combination, or simply, the Syndicate—had Americanized the Mafia, also known as the Italian Organization, the Black Hand and later, La Cosa Nostra. The Depression had de-ethnicized organized crime and made it, instead, a way of life for anyone with the tenacity to rob, cheat, lie, muscle and kill. Unlike the Mafia, membership in the Syndicate was open. But like the Mafia, once a member, always a member.

While the Depression had presented opportunities to a national mob of organized thugs, organized crime in America had thrived since the turn of the century. As immigrants poured into the promised land of opportunity and settled in the big city slums, grassroots bullies muscled their way to power. In the larger cities, like New York, gangs of fratellos (hoods) elected a capo whom they obeyed as the boss of their borgato (family). The bosses selected their consigliari (counsellors) and elected the capo de tutti capi (boss of all bosses). In essence, fratellos conducted each borgato's business, which usually included shakedowns, numbers writing, prostitution, narcotics and booze. Each borgato was confined to its own district, and crossing family lines was taboo. Opportunists operated in every borgato, however, and feuds were often settled by the capo de tutti capi or by bullets.

In the twenties and thirties, when the Mafia was supreme among America's criminal classes, gangland murders in Chicago, New York and Cleveland were screamed across the front pages of the nation's press. "One-way rides" and shoot-outs on street corners, in restaurants and in barber shops became frequent occurrences as the Mafiosi struggled for power and wealth. In 1924 in Chicago, Irish gangster Dion O'Banion was gunned down in his flower shop after he had interfered with the Sicilian Genna Brothers who were pushing their rot-gut whiskey in O'Banion territory.

Four years later, in the same vicious city, gang leader Al Capone was gunning for rival gangster Bugs Moran. The hunt resulted in the St. Valentine's Day Massacre of six men in a Chicago warehouse. They were riddled by machine-gun fire and then shot individually as they lay bleeding on the floor. Moran, however, was not among the slain hoods.

In New York, on April 15, 1931, some fratellos of Vito Genovese, malicious lieutenant of Lucky Luciano, gunned down Joe "the Boss" Masseria in a Brooklyn restaurant. Later that year, as part of the same power struggle which eventually put Luciano in charge of the Mafia, gang boss Salvatore Maranzano took four gunshot blasts and five stab wounds before he died in his plush Manhattan office.

The bad publicity that followed each gangland murder brought "heat" from the feds and interfered with business, as the Mafia realized by the mid-1930s. So following Maranzano's murder the Mafia called a reconciliatory "sit-down" for Chicago. There it was decided that the position, capo de tutti capi, would be abolished as it created jealousy among the family bosses. In its place, the Mafia instituted a national authority or commission—the Big Seven. It included families from New York, Brooklyn, Chicago and Cleveland whose capos were considered equals and as such, policymakers. The most powerful of capos was Luciano. His power, however, was not independent of the Big Seven, who also cooperated with the National Crime Syndicate, including the murderous outfits of Meyer Lansky and John "the Fox" Torrio. United, the new American Mob could generate ample power and money for all.

A second event which contributed to the Americanization of the Mafia was the Depression. The architects of the American Mob trusted in the economic theory of supply and demand. It had worked for them for several decades. Now, following Black Tuesday, there existed in America an unrivaled demand for cash. And this was the turning point for the American Mob, which was by no measure short of money. Bootlegging had produced millions of dollars for organized criminals and the Depression had unexpectedly given them the opportunity to plant their money where it would yield the ripest returns. Following the crash on Wall Street, thousands of businessmen flocked to the only source of money and credit: the American Mob. They came begging, these businessmen, and they walked away with operating capital and, most importantly to the Mob, life-time partners. Within three years, organized crime had infiltrated America's big businesses.

As if that weren't enough, organized criminals, during the same era that they became "businessmen," also became "politicians." Mob money filled the campaign coffers that had previously been stuffed by businessmen. In return for their money, the mobsters were guaranteed a lucrative future. What was once a country in which the mobster was a lower class citizen now abruptly became a country in which the mobster was king.

Like all major cities, Pittsburgh had its share of kings. One of them was David L. Lawrence who served as Governor of the State of Pennsylvania from 1959 to 1963. Before that he had served several terms as Mayor of Pittsburgh and also many years as the state's Democratic National Committeeman.

While Lawrence was never convicted of any wrongdoing, his reputation was tainted by the company he kept and by his political activities. Once, he was about to be indicted in western Pennsylvania for a scandal involving a Pittsburgh contract that was awarded to his Allegheny Asphalt Company. At the time, Lawrence was the Democratic National Committeeman and he allegedly convinced an assistant United States attorney to fix the grand jury. Lawrence was not indicted and the attorney shortly thereafter was appointed to a judgeship and later to the Common Pleas Court.

Lawrence's rise to power followed the end of the Hoover GOP and the prevailing resentment of the Depression. In 1932 he helped engineer the presidential nomination of Franklin D. Roosevelt. In his own state, that year, Lawrence knew every single victor on the national, state and local tickets because he had either personally put them on "his" party ballot or he had a voice in so doing.

Lawrence served as the party's national committeeman

with Emma Guffey Miller, the sharp-tongued but brilliant sister of the then United States Senator Joseph Guffey. While he supported Mrs. Miller publicly, privately Lawrence hated both her and her brother because they prevented him from exercising complete control over "his" party.

Despite the Guffeys, Lawrence managed to "make" justices, judges, governors and senators and eventually he earned the epithet "Maker of Presidents." Besides his role in the Roosevelt nomination, Lawrence was credited for a part in winning the Vice Presidential nod for Harry S. Truman in 1944. Then, in 1960, Governor Lawrence, a Catholic, was instrumental in helping John F. Kennedy win Pennsylvania by nearly 120,000 votes.

Lawrence was not content to be national committeeman for he feared that the large protestant majorities in Pennsylvania would prevent him from capturing any state or national elective offices. So he satisfied his thirst for power by "owning" the men whom he put in those seats.

In the late 1940s, however, Lawrence was perplexed about selecting a candidate for Pittsburgh's mayoral race. He had searched among the likely candidates for the man of his liking, but wasn't able to find one. Accordingly, he decided to "take" the nomination himself and gamble his power. He was elected and later re-elected twice before his successful campaign for the Governor's mansion.

Throughout Lawrence's incumbency as mayor and governor, he relied on loyal party hacks, collectors and payrollers, all of whom were accustomed to calling him by his more appropriate appellation, "the boss." Among this group was James Spagnola, known as Jimmy Spankard, Lawrence's chairman in the first and third wards of Pittsburgh. Spankard, some said, collected for "the boss" from the racket-controlled wards for more than twenty years, until an enterprising reporter discovered that the powerful ward chairman was not a citizen of the United States. He had even been voting illegally! Unembarrassed, Lawrence replaced his man, but Spagnola escaped prosecution.

Lawrence was struck down by a heart attack in 1966 while he addressed a Democratic rally, and died within a few days. His death left a power vacuum in Pennsylvanian politics.

While Lawrence was never directly linked to another of Pittsburgh's kings, John Sebastian LaRocca, he certainly was aware of the young hoodlum's influence and power in Pittsburgh. LaRocca was Pittsburgh's Mafia success story, a master at weaving the political opportunities of his time into curtains of gold which shut out the law and insulated him against everyday responsibilities of citizenship, or even the pangs of conscience.

Born in Italy in 1903, LaRocca came to the United States when he was ten years old. By the age of twenty-one he was sent to prison for assault with intent to kill. Later, he was convicted for carrying concealed weapons and, most humiliating of all, operating a numbers racket. In 1939, during a numbers raid, LaRocca was caught in the alley behind his numbers payoff headquarters. Inside, detectives found an adding machine, a trunk full of numbers slips and a bureau drawer jammed with money, amounting to $3,430.

Big John LaRocca got his start as a moonshiner and numbers boss in the East Liberty section of Pittsburgh. Until 1932, he was a subordinate of Southwestern Pennsylvania's first Mafia boss, John Bazzano, Sr., a Sicilian immigrant who had arrived in the 1890s.

Bazzano ordered the 1929 execution of three brothers of a rival gang in Pittsburgh, after a jurisdictional dispute in that city's bootlegging underworld. Two of the brothers survived and carried their complaint to their capo. In 1932, Bazzano was lured to a Brooklyn testimonial dinner in his honor, and there he was stabbed to death with icepicks. Back in Pittsburgh, John Sebastian LaRocca became "the boss."

With his take from the rackets, LaRocca acquired a cement block company, a beverage firm, some real estate, a car wash, and linen and clothing interests. Among his "business" associates were Lucky Luciano in Italy and Sammy Mannarino in Cuba. "The Rock" also "owned" political fixers and underworld silencers who wielded awesome authority in city, state and national political organizations.

In 1953, LaRocca's petition for citizenship was pending when the United States Immigration and Naturalization Service discovered that he had been convicted of two crimes of moral turpitude. LaRocca had the 1922 assault charges against him plus a later conviction for stealing automobile plates. On such grounds, "the Rock" could be deported. However, the Government's attempt to deport him as an undesirable alien was thwarted when Pennsylvania's corrupt Governor John S. Fine pardoned the gangster's larceny conviction.

LaRocca was allegedly among the sixty war lords who in 1957 met at the home of Joseph Barbara in the New York village of Apalachin. Big John, Kelly Mannarino, brother of Sam, and Michael Genovese were delegates to the meeting from the Pittsburgh area. The purpose of the gathering has never been ascertained but many of the guests were arrested when police raided Barbara's home. LaRocca was one of the gangsters who escaped the mountaintop rendezvous, but Mannarino and Genovese were trapped.

As early as the mid-1940s, John Sebastian LaRocca was recognized by J. Edgar Hoover, as the boss of a sordid army of pimps, shake-down artists, bookies, dope peddlers and politician-corrupters who operated in the tri-state area of Southwestern Pennsylvania, contiguous eastern Ohio and the industrial border towns of West Virginia. LaRocca's army, according to the late Andrew T. Park, then District Attorney of Allegheny County, numbered more than 20,000 men. By the 1970s, the Pennsylvania Crime Commission continued to identify the surly and fleshy-lipped LaRocca, then in his seventies, as the head of Southwestern Pennsylvania's organized crime operations.

There were other kings in Pittsburgh at the time Andrew J. Susce was hired by the Bureau of Internal Revenue, but none of them operated politically without the sanction of David L. Lawrence or criminally without the personal approval of John Sebastian LaRocca. The correlation between political and criminal activity in Pittsburgh, as evidenced by the long history of prosecutions of venal civil servants in that city, gives reason to believe that LaRocca conducted his business at the pleasure of David Leo Lawrence and vice versa. Pittsburgh, in the 1940s and before, was a city where gambling, prostitution and other illegal operations were conducted openly and freely. Where such conditions existed, warned the late Senator Hubert H. Humphrey, who in the 1940s was Mayor of Minneapolis, "You can be sure the chief of police and probably the mayor, too, is on the take."

Between the late 1930s and 1943, there were continual allegations that police officials and other public servants in Pittsburgh, including then Mayor Cornelius D. Scully, were in the pockets of the Mob. Despite these allegations and a number of dismissals and convictions, which were front page stories in the Pittsburgh dailies, Pittsburgh remained firmly in the grip of organized crime. In the eleventh, twelfth and thirteenth wards, the numbers racket operated as openly as the legal lotteries of a later era. While Andrew Susce canvassed the wards in pursuit of tax delinquent businessmen, he frequently witnessed bets being placed in taverns, cigar stores and pool rooms.

Susce knew that the rackets were illegal, but the numbers business was not within his jurisdiction. He was a tax assessor and collector, not a police officer. He didn't play the numbers himself, but he knew that in his wards, as well as throughout Pittsburgh, the illegal lottery was routine. In fact, it was estimated in the mid-1940s that more than 300,000 persons played the numbers every day in Pittsburgh. By 1975, the Pennsylvania Crime Commission estimated that the gambling rackets alone netted the Mob an annual profit of $120 million. And John Sebastian LaRocca, hidden behind a wall of police protection, controlled it all.

In Susce's opinion J. Edgar Hoover had a right, even an obligation, to request an investigation of John Sebastian LaRocca, who undoubtedly was bilking the Government as Pittsburgh's number one racketeer. But for Granger and O'Malley to expect a Zone Deputy Collector to penetrate the LaRocca combine was, in Susce's mind, an outrageous request. It was senseless. The Mob was insulated and it would take months of probing by the agency's best investigators to come up with anything concrete against John "the Rock." Even then, as had been the case with other gangsters who had been investigated in Pittsburgh, the charges would be watered down or dismissed. Rarely would any money be collected. Consequently, tax employees, who had to meet a monthly quota of tax collections to protect their jobs, shied away from investigating racketeers.

In April, 1943, however, Andrew J. Susce braced himself. He could not, he had decided, settle for a whitewash. He would penetrate the LaRocca combine and he would insist that his report be forwarded to the bureau's Intelligence Division so that it could be further investigated and then submitted to the FBI.

Susce's probe, which was to take nine months, began on the day he visited James Angotti, a handsome young numbers writer who ran a tobacco shop on Elmwood Avenue in Homewood, just east of East Liberty. Angotti, unknown to Susce, had been a bookkeeper for the LaRocca combine.

"Jim," Susce said when he entered Angotti's shop, "I've got a problem and you can help me."

"What's the problem, Andy, and I'll see what I can do."

Angotti considered Susce a friend whom he had often consulted about tax problems.

"Do you know John Sebastian LaRocca?"

"Sure I do. Why?"

"I've been assigned to investigate him for tax evasion," Susce whispered, "but I don't know where to begin. Can you help me?"

Angotti invited Susce into the back of his shop where he ran his numbers operation. "Andy," he said pointing to his numbers slips, "LaRocca is the banker. I'm obligated to him. But if you need some information, I'll give you the books that I've kept for the combine. Don't say where you got 'em, understand, and don't ask me for no more information."

"But what if they ask you for the books?"

"Don't worry, I'll say I lost 'em." Angotti handed Susce three leather-bound ledgers and the agent stuffed them into his briefcase before leaving the shop.

Back at the Federal Building, careful not to let anyone see what he had, Susce examined the contents of the books. They covered several years of the numbers operation that was run by Angotti and dozens of other writers in the LaRocca combine. Included in the books were dates, names of writers and collectors, plus turn-in points and amounts of dollars collected. In a matter of hours Susce determined that LaRocca's tax returns, retrieved from Washington, were fraudulent. LaRocca had not declared thousands of dollars of income.

Susce was pleased, confident that he was on the right track, but he wanted more evidence. He decided to check out several of the names that appeared in the book. At least one of the names, Joseph Gigliotti, was familiar to the investigator. He was one of the area's wealthiest racketeers, and was a terror. Always dressed like a prominent banker, Gigliotti was a collector for the LaRocca combine. Early in Susce's bureau career, he had investigated one of Gigliotti's tax returns and proved it fraudulent. The difference between the actual amount earned and the amount declared was trifling and Gigliotti paid his debt without a fuss. In the field, among businessmen in Susce's wards, Gigliotti was feared and loathed. He considered everyone his puppet, and when he got the urge to open a new numbers station, he approached whoever he thought would be the most productive man for the combine. If that person was uncooperative, Gigliotti applied pressure, and he wasn't above physical harassment or torching a business to get his way.

This explained why Angotti, who had occasionally suffered at Gigliotti's hand, cooperated with Susce. Angotti knew that LaRocca's protection was too thick for Susce to penetrate, but if he could hurt Gigliotti, then "losing" the books was worth it. Susce thought it would be foolish for him to visit Gigliotti. That would create more of a stir than necessary. But he was sure that when he turned over Angotti's books to the Intelligence boys, Gigliotti would be one of the first racketeers nailed.

There was another name in Angotti's books that interested Susce: that of Joseph Brusco. Susce had first heard the name when he visited Joe Lewis, another small-time racketeer who was a numbers writer in the LaRocca combine. Susce had helped Lewis file his returns on several occasions. Susce told Lewis about the bureau investigation of LaRocca, and asked Lewis for advice.

"Get to Brusco," Lewis told the field agent. "Joe Brusco is LaRocca's partner and if he talks you've got a case."

Susce figured the chances of Brusco talking were as remote as John Sebastian LaRocca turning himself in, but just the same he went to Brusco's home in East Liberty. He knocked at the wooden door and it was opened by a wiry gentleman of medium height who appeared to be in his early forties.

"Can I help ya?" asked the man, softly.

"Yes sir, I'm looking for Joseph Brusco."

"I'm Mr. Brusco. Who are you?"

"I'm Andrew J. Susce, Zone Deputy Collector of the United States Bureau of Internal Revenue," said the visitor, his field credentials extended.

"I've heard of you boys, whatta ya want from me?"

"Mr. Brusco, I need some information."

"What kind of information?" Brusco's face was impassive.

"I'm investigating John Sebastian LaRocca and I know that you're one of his partners," Susce said.

"How do you know that?" Brusco asked. His face remained expressionless.

"It's not important how I know it, Mr. Brusco. I know it. I need information about LaRocca and the numbers racket in East Liberty."

"Jesus Christ, man," Brusco suddenly shouted. "Are you crazy? I'll go to hell before I'll give you that kind of information."

"Mr. Brusco," Susce interrupted, "I don't blame you. If you don't want to tell me, I can't force you. But if you ever change your mind, I'm in the Federal Building. Look me up."

Susce had hoped that Brusco might cooperate with him or lead him to the concrete information he was after. But since he had balked, there was nothing for Susce to do but write the report with the information he had collected.

When he analyzed the combine books, Susce had estimated that LaRocca's combine had raked in more than $180 million in the numbers business in the several years covered by the ledgers.

"That's just scratching the surface," Susce told his superior, William P. O'Malley. "Bill, this is big money fraud. I need a Special Agent to assist me in this investigation. We can make cases."

O'Malley refused Susce's request. "Write the report and get it in, Andy," was the advice O'Malley gave to the Zone Deputy Collector.

Not long afterwards, while Susce was at his desk writing the report, a secretary informed him that he had a visitor.

"He wouldn't give me his name," she told the field agent, "but he's mean-looking."

Susce walked to the lobby and was startled. There stood Joseph Brusco.

"Mr. Brusco," Susce said as he extended his hand. "Come to pay some taxes?"

"I want to see you," Brusco said.

"What about?"

"You want to know about John LaRocca?"

"But you said—"

"I changed my mind, Susce. I got a statement to make."

Confused, Susce asked Brusco to be seated. He went back to his desk and phoned the office of George Meshank, then United States attorney in Pittsburgh. Certain that O'Malley wouldn't provide an agent to assist him in taking Brusco's confession, Susce hoped Meshank would help him. But the United States attorney wasn't any more cooperative than O'Malley. He did, however, inform Susce to advise Brusco to contact his attorney. He also told him that if he took a statement from Brusco, it should be under oath and in the presence of another field agent.

Susce then arranged for a government stenographer to record the confession and he also asked Gene Panneton, a Zone Deputy Collector, to witness the confession. Dressed in a tailored suit, Brusco was ushered into a conference room where he selected a seat at the end of a rectangular table. Susce took his place at the opposite end. As Brusco placed his hat on one corner of the table, Susce advised him to call an attorney.

"I don't need my attorney," was the quiet response.

Susce swore-in Brusco and asked him to say what he came to say. Four hours later, without breaking for lunch, Brusco picked up his hat and left the conference room. He had revealed numerous violations of the income tax laws by public officials. Specifically, Brusco told Susce that he operated a numbers station from his home and that his daily take of about $200 was turned over to John LaRocca. Furthermore, Brusco said there were eight other lieutenants in the LaRocca combine who were turning in daily receipts to "the Rock." Several of the lieutenants brought in thousands of dollars each, every day.

Brusco also put the finger on David L. Lawrence, who, he claimed, protected the rackets as Pennsylvania's Democratic National Committeeman. According to Brusco, Lawrence "appointed the right people" to protect the Mob. Pittsburgh's Mayor Cornelius D. Scully, Brusco alleged, took his orders from Lawrence and Lawrence's associate, James P. Kirk, County Chairman. These men, claimed Brusco, were paid protection fees by the LaRocca combine.

Brusco told Susce that LaRocca paid $1,000 a week in protection money to Charles "the Pope" Papale, a vocal alderman and magistrate in East Liberty who answered to Mayor Scully. As head of the twelfth ward, Papale brought in three strong-arm men to run the rackets, bank the take and discipline errant numbersmen and runners. Because they were so rapacious, the trio was tagged, "The Three Pigs." One of the three was John Sebastian LaRocca.

In 1939, Papale resigned under fire from the Scully administration when he was accused of "whitewashing" numbers operators who were arrested in East Liberty. Mayor Scully himself had suspended the magistrate. However, Papale told his barber, "I'll be taken care of, I'm a close friend of the Mayor's." Sure enough, a few weeks later, Mayor Scully shifted around his Democratic employees in order to appoint Papale to the Board of Mercantile Appraisers at an annual salary of $5,000—$1,000 more than his salary as magistrate.

As Brusco explained it, Papale was still "on the take" in East Liberty, although his share diminished after he resigned.

Brusco also told Susce that Gus Ellis, John Flavin and John Hudak, all police inspectors, were "doing business with LaRocca" and helping him build the numbers and slot machine businesses in East Liberty. These men, Brusco testified, also received weekly payoffs for protection.

In addition to the police officials, Brusco revealed that Churchill Mehard, Mayor Scully's City Solicitor, and George Meshner, mystery man at City Hall who was the go-between for the Mayor and the Mob, were also receiving weekly protection fees.

Following Brusco's unexpected confession, Susce made a second appeal for a Special Agent to assist him in the LaRocca probe. This time he put his request in writing to O'Malley and Granger as well. Again, the request was denied and Susce was urged to turn in his report. But Susce wasn't forgetting O'Malley's earlier advice to be thorough and to take whatever time he needed to complete the report. He decided he wasn't ready to write it yet.

Brusco's confession had revealed more than Susce had hoped for. Why he came forward, Susce would never know. There was speculation, however, that Brusco and LaRocca had had a quarrel. Going to the Feds could have been Brusco's retaliation. Whatever the circumstances, Susce realized he was now riding an investigation that exposed not only widespread criminal corruption in Pittsburgh, but also a national Syndicate. In response to Susce's question, "Is John Sebastian LaRocca a member of an organized Mob that operates throughout this country?" Brusco had nodded his head, "Yes." Susce was appalled.

The FBI had emphatically stated that the existence of an

organized Mob in the United States was ludicrous. But here was Andrew Susce, a Zone Deputy Collector in one of America's great industrial cities, with information that the FBI was wrong. He wondered if anyone would listen to his incredible story, much less believe it. He knew that he had hard facts and that what he had could be substantiated. Now nothing could divert him from his course.

Progress on the investigation was slowed, however, when Susce suddenly began receiving routine assignments to complete in addition to the LaRocca probe. Rumor had it that someone in the Bureau of Internal Revenue had uncovered information about the local Mob, and the Bureau was being pressured to keep the information "in house." Nonetheless, Susce spent the remainder of the summer of 1943, and the early fall, chasing leads that Brusco had furnished. Often, in order to complete his assignments, Susce took the LaRocca investigation home with him and worked on it in the evenings.

By October, 1943, Susce was ready to write his report. Before he began, however, he wanted to meet face to face with LaRocca. Why? Even if he would see the field agent it was doubtful that he would cooperate in his own investigation. But this late in the probe, after he had already been surprised by Angotti and Brusco, Susce thought he should risk the visit. Through the gangster's personal accountant, Susce arranged a meeting.

The first thing Susce noticed when he met John LaRocca was the racketeer's youth. He was a powerful man, but he was only forty in 1943. Trim, groomed to his finger tips and impeccably dressed, LaRocca was amiable. Suddenly Susce understood the stories he'd heard about LaRocca being "loved" by his neighbors. "The Rock" was indeed a gentleman, at least on the surface.

LaRocca smiled graciously as Susce explained the reason

for his visit. "Mr. Susce," the gangster said, "I'll cooperate with you in whatever way you request."

The kindness frightened Susce. He had expected some resistance. "Well I certainly appreciate that, Mr. LaRocca."

Without batting an eye, LaRocca smiled and complimented Susce. He said he had known of the investigation for some time. "I want to tell you something, Mr. Susce. I got no quarrel with the United States government. I love this country. Whatever tax I owe, I'll pay. Just let me know what I owe you, and I'll pay. But I must warn ya that I'm broke."

LaRocca seemed to understand that the quickest way to end the probe was to pay some back taxes.

Susce's tax mind was sharper than LaRocca imagined. His job was to *investigate* LaRocca. He was not told to collect any tax money. He knew that if he picked up a cent of LaRocca's money, he would jeopardize the government's case against the gangster and preclude any further investigation by the Intelligence Division. John LaRocca had admitted willful fraud; that was more than Susce had expected, and he would settle for it.

"Mr. LaRocca, thank you for your time and your cooperation. I'll make my report to my superiors and I'm sure you'll hear from us." Susce left the meeting.

LaRocca may have been surprised that Susce didn't jump at the chance to assess his income, but he was not frightened by Susce's parting words. LaRocca knew that he had a fix above Agent Susce's head. What he didn't know, however, was that Andrew J. Susce would haunt him for the rest of his life.

CHAPTER THREE

# The Report

When Stanley Granger opened the envelope containing J. Edgar Hoover's request for an investigation of the business of John Sebastian LaRocca, he knew it was a case for Robert Cory's Intelligence Division. Cory's Special Agents were trained for such complex investigations. They had collected millions of dollars in delinquent taxes and made cases against notorious hoods like Al Capone. The least qualified candidate for such an investigation, Granger also knew, was a Zone Deputy Collector whose routine obligations required only minimal training. But in 1943, Granger was aware of the entanglements and mass firings that would follow within the tax agency and the city government if LaRocca were as successfully investigated as Capone had been.

Since it would clearly be unthinkable and equally suspicious to refuse Hoover's request, Granger had no choice but to order the LaRocca probe. But Zone Deputy Collector Susce, and not one of Cory's boys, would be his man for the job. The right man, Granger figured, to come up empty handed, or at the most make an inconsequential tax assessment against Big John. Granger had quite mistakenly pegged Susce for a patsy who, if requested, would "fix" his report to "protect" the agency and its employees. Certainly Susce would "protect" himself thought the Collector. He had a family to feed. The idea never entered Granger's mind that Susce was a man with a self-image of honesty and incorruptibility.

Susce's meeting with LaRocca marked the end of his lengthy probe. All that remained to be done was to turn in the written report. This would require several weeks' work. Susce intended to prove that not only was John Sebastian LaRocca delinquent in his tax payments, but that the mobster's forces had penetrated the highest elective offices in the City of Pittsburgh and the State of Pennsylvania, and in doing so had corrupted policemen, aldermen, judges, lawyers, private citizens and federal agents who promoted and protected the LaRocca combine. Furthermore, Susce wanted to show that LaRocca was a member of an organized gang of hoodlums that had national and international influence, permitting them to deal in narcotics, booze, gambling, prostitution and racketeering from Cuba to Florida to Ontario with operations in between in Detroit, Cleveland, Pittsburgh, Buffalo and New York City.

Susce recognized his shortcomings as an investigator, a job for which he had little training, so he decided to write his report as completely and convincingly as possible, but always with the understanding that he was merely leading the way for a later, more comprehensive investigation of the LaRocca combine. He felt that the information he had uncovered would arouse action by the bureau's tax officials in Washington, D.C., so that a team of Special Agents would be ordered to follow-up his preliminary probe.

Armed with the confession of Joseph Brusco, from which half of his report would be written, plus the books given to him by Angotti and information gathered from various other sources, including a police magistrate and ward leaders, Susce began writing.

"Introduction to Criminal Investigation and Finding of Facts Relating to the Income of John LaRocca et al. Part One. Re: the Bureau Investigation of Sebastino LaRocca, alias John Sebastian LaRocca, alias John LaRoc, alias Lester LaRocco, alias the Pig.

"It is endeavored to be shown herein that Sebastian LaRocca et al. has wilfully, knowingly and intentionally defrauded the United States Government of income tax by fraudulently and criminally omitting and falsifying income from illegal methods of operation, and that by doing so Sebastin LaRocca committed gross indignities against the United States and should stand trial for same."

With those words, Andrew J. Susce opened his 300-page document which would include thirty-seven exhibits ranging from the Brusco confession and the numbers books of Angotti to photostatic copies of income tax returns of LaRocca, bank deposits of the LaRocca combine, photographs of gangsters from police files, and press clippings from the Pittsburgh newspapers and the *Bulletin Index,* a city magazine which consistently carried charges of criminal connections between Pittsburgh's politicians and racketeers.

In the opening pages of the report, Susce further alleged that he had calculated a take (income) of ten million dollars per year by the LaRocca combine and that more than $180 million of syndicate income had escaped liability for tax with the knowledge and acquiescence of many of the officials in the Pittsburgh tax bureau.

Susce ascertained that while he had found LaRocca delinquent, "Jeopardy assessments were not prepared because permission for a Special Agent was refused and I was not going to damage the government case by preparing the same. I saw fraud and discontinued immediately."

He further reported that "John Sebastino [*sic*] La Rocca has put everyone under the impression that he is out of the numbers business and that he is broke. That is an illusion. LaRocca is still active in the numbers business. Michael Genovese is the man who is picking up the numbers for LaRocca and [George] Messner [the go-between for the Mob and City Hall]. This information was given to me this month by James Angotti, the former combine secretary for the East Liberty numbers men. Mr. Angotti is at present actively engaged in the numbers business on Homewood Avenue in a place called Jimmy's. Across the street from Jimmy's is Al Pierce's Book Shop, backed up by Messner, who is a partner of John LaRocca."

Allegations were fired at LaRocca throughout the 300-page report, but Exhibit A, the confession of Brusco, was the most damaging to LaRocca and his combine. Susce wrote that Brusco confessed that he was a co-partner of LaRocca and that he had lived in East Liberty, Pa., for thirty-two years. Brusco said that LaRocca purchased a new automobile every year in addition to quantities of tailored clothes. "He [LaRocca] has at least 1,000 ties at home, each worth $5.00."

With Brusco's help, Susce zeroed in on LaRocca's income from 1937 to 1940. "Notice the income of Sebastian John LaRocca for 1937, stated by the co-partner (Brusco) to be $28,000 (from the numbers racket alone). Sebastian LaRocca made a return for the year 1937 in the amount of $3,600.00. This is a difference in calculation of $24,400.00."

The following year, according to Susce, LaRocca's take from the East Liberty rackets was $42,000 but in 1938 LaRocca had reported a slim $4,050 in income. "Kindly notice that 1938 was a better year on account of better police protection. This is not to be lost sight of . . ."

For the year 1939, LaRocca reported earning $4,737.50, but Brusco and Susce estimated the racketeer had grossed in excess of $56,000.

The next year, 1940, "was a year in which income tax evasion can be easily proved. Up to September 1940 the income of Sebastian LaRocca was $30,000. LaRocca reported $10,708.60 . . . Sebastian kept no records, so the flat figure must have come from a mere estimate." Susce said LaRocca's actual income for 1940 was more than $50,000, including $30,000 earned from the numbers racket and $18,750 from his coin machines. "This is the year in which LaRocca brought out his one-arm bandits. He made a minimum of $30 per week on each machine. There was $750 minimum take per week from his machines. He was in the slot machine business about twenty-five weeks of the year . . ."

Susce's report was not entirely humorless as he pointed out inconsistencies in LaRocca's claims about his status of citizenship. "In 1938 as per income tax return, LaRocca checked off that he was a citizen of the United States, whereas he is an alien. On his 1937 return he swore he was an alien . . . to this day John LaRocca is not a citizen . . . Again in his 1939 return LaRocca swears he is an alien." He did likewise in 1940, two years after he had already claimed to be a citizen.

There were also deductions allowed for expenses on LaRocca's returns. "Note the entertainment expense (in 1939) of $520. How silly to allow entertainment deductions for a numbers writer. This return was reviewed and approved . . . (in 1940). Note that again LaRocca reported $520 for entertaining exemption. What kind of entertaining does a numbers man do?"

Susce also argued that "There is no bonafide reason for the support of his niece Agnes, which he claims in his income tax return (for 1940)."

While Zone Deputy Collector Susce blackened LaRocca's name, he also caught his tax superiors in an embarrassing situation. William McCartney was a United States Deputy Collector reporting to Stanley Granger, Collector. McCartney was the Mob's man in the tax bureau and another of Granger's "yes" men. He threatened to kill Susce's report prior to it reaching the Intelligence Division. He also promised to have Susce transferred to another office. This same William McCartney was the tax agent who had prepared and authorized the tax returns of John Sebastian LaRocca in the years 1936, 1937 and 1938.

"Kindly notice that on each return Sebastian LaRocca lists himself as a numbers operator, not writer or pick up man. This United States Deputy Collector (McCartney) told me that he personally knew Sebastian LaRocca and that LaRocca came directly to him (for tax assistance). Notice that the income tax returns of LaRocca were not marked for investigation as is always the custom under similar circumstances. This is the same United States Deputy Collector who covered up Charles Papale (the powerful ward chairman and racketeer) and who would not permit me to question him. This is the same Papale who gave protection to LaRocca. It seems that something is peculiarly wrong when a man who is working for the United States government prevents a United States (Zone) Deputy Collector from questioning a suspected income tax evader . . . It should be noticed that the co-partner of Sebastian LaRocca states under oath that John LaRocca paid protection money to Charles Papale, alias Charles the Pope."

Susce further wrote, "I am of the opinion that the returns prepared for LaRocca by William McCartney are fraudulent and should be referred to the Intelligence Division. I am of the opinion that William McCartney, on orders of William P. O'Malley the United States Chief Deputy, are [sic] aiding and abetting the racketeers." Later in the report, Susce wrote, "McCartney knew LaRocca was a numbers operator but did not indicate that the returns for 1936, 1937 and 1938 should have gone to the Intelligence Bureau as is customary."

Even the tax returns of confessed racketeer Brusco didn't

escape Susce's suspicious eyes. "Special attention should be given to the returns of Joseph Brusco, alias Joseph Brisk. This man filed his returns with United States Deputy Collector William McCartney, the federal protector of the rackets . . . Mr. William McCartney did not permit me to prepare the returns for Joseph Brusco because Brusco is a personal friend of Jack Fitzgerald, who is a nephew of David Lawrence . . . Mr. McCartney told me that Joseph Brusco was the big fish and that he was going to handle his affairs. That he was going to prepare the income tax returns for Brusco."

To the further embarrassment and ire of his superiors, Susce also charged, "It is to be remarked that when a fraud case is found William McCartney, on orders from William P. O'Malley, sees to it that the investigation never reaches the Intelligence Division. Mr. Cory, Chief of the Intelligence Division, invariably seems to take the word of McCartney."

Later in the report, Susce explained that McCartney had ordered him not to pursue collection of $1,500 in delinquent taxes from a Pittsburgh racketeer who had fled to California. The racketeer offered a compromise payment of $25. "I was instructed by Mr. William McCartney, the United States Deputy, not to prepare a letter of refusal on this offer in compromise. It is very unusual that a United States employee should protect a racketeer."

McCartney and O'Malley were only two of more than two dozen tax officials, city officials and racketeers who felt Susce's sting. As Susce dug into LaRocca's business concerns, particularly the Twentieth Century Towel Supply Corporation, he uncovered details about Big John's fraudulent schemes and implicated several of his friends and business associates. "Notice especially the minutes of the Corporation," Susce wrote in Exhibit B, Minutes of Twentieth Century Towel Corporation. "Kindly take notice of the fact that this was a blind corporation. The real purpose behind this corporation was the numbers business . . . the man who is behind the Twentieth Century Towel Supply Co. is George Messner, this is the secret partner. Also notice that the corporation had offices at 6200 Penn Ave., in the Negley Building. It is very unusual to have a Laundry Company in a general office building. Notice also that the corporation did its banking business not in East Liberty where there were two large banking institutions, but they did their banking in Homewood, that is in the Homewood Bank on Homewood Avenue. This is to be noted because the home of George Messner, the main backer of this combine, is in the Homewood District. This Twentieth Century Towel Corporation has connections in New York City and other principal cities such as Cleveland, Steubenville, Detroit and Miami. LaRocca and Messner make frequent trips to Detroit and Miami. Both have recently returned from New York, Florida and Michigan."

Messner, the go-between for the Mob and City Hall, had allegedly told Susce that while the corporation was a cover-up for LaRocca's numbers racket, the racket was protected by Harvey Scott, Police Superintendent, who took orders from Pittsburgh Mayor Cornelius Scully. "The Mayor receives his orders from [David] Lawrence or James P. Kirk," Susce wrote. He later explained that Messner, a long-time acquaintance and business partner of LaRocca, related to him that "it was possible for the Chief Executive of the City of Pittsburgh, Mayor Scully, to be mixed up in the numbers combine . . . Has Mayor Scully's income tax returns [sic] been checked for illegal income?" Susce wondered. Furthermore, "Does David Leo Lawrence report his income received from the rackets? Does Mr. Kirk?"

Concerning Police Superintendent Scott, Susce wrote, "[He] was a life-long resident of Homewood until he became Superintendent. He was pledged to clean up the numbers racket in Pittsburgh when he took office. Under him the situation has grown from bad to worse . . . He wormed himself into the confidence of the Department of Justice while all the time he was giving aid and assistance to the numbers men . . . Has Mr. Scott declared his income from these illegal operations?" In the Angotti books there was mention of a $300-per-week payment to "some high city official," and Susce said he thought the "official" was Scott.

The original incorporators of the Twentieth Century Towel Supply Corporation, according to Susce's records, were George C. Reilly, Edwin E. Lindgren, John Cosgrove and Harry C. Hand, all of New York City. "It is self evident that these men came from New York to Pennsylvania to organize an illegal corporation under the heading of the Twentieth Century Towel Supply Corporation and here it was a part of a numbers syndicate. Kindly take cognizance of the fact that these men were the associates of John S. LaRocca in the good old bootlegging days when John LaRocca made plenty of money—and he did not report this money on his income tax returns."

Susce had obtained information about the towel corporation from Dun and Bradstreet as well as from the corporation's bank and Social Security records. Of the Dun and Bradstreet information Susce wrote, "Notice that John LaRocca claims himself to be a naturalized citizen, and in the United States District Court he is applying for United States Citizenship. Notice also that he specifically states that he was in the olive oil and grape businesses for fifteen years; where are the profits from the operations? . . . Notice under method of operation that when the Towel Supply Corporation started, in 1940, there were 75 active accounts at two dollars per month, namely $150 per month—for twelve months $1800 . . . It is physically impossible to show $35,000 in deposits in the Homewood Bank and only charge two dollars per month for the service. There is a hidden account, namely numbers, and this corporation was actively engaged in the illegal operation of numbers, etc."

Susce was not satisfied that he had all "the goods" on the Towel Supply Corporation until he visited the company's offices. "A careful examination revealed that the laundry company had wash tubs, but all that ever was discovered in the nature of any clothes to be cleaned were cobwebs. This indicates that at no time were there clothes or laundry to be cleaned but that the main hidden asset behind the Laundry Company was the numbers racket. An officer of the People's Pittsburgh Trust Company refused a loan for the purpose of buying a truck because it was a shady corporation, and he [the loan officer] had his doubts if they were conducting a legal business."

Susce linked two other LaRocca associates to the Twentieth Century Towel Supply Corporation: Joseph Gigliotti, the sadistic numbers collector, and Sammy Mannarino, who was into dope, numbers, prostitution, slot machines and gambling, owning an exclusive casino in Ontario, Canada, "which does a half million dollar business per year." Susce wrote, "John LaRocca, Joseph Gigliotti and Sammy Mannarino are inseparable pals along with George Messner. Messner is the boy who secures the police protection for the boys. He is exceedingly close to all the big boys in the country and the city and he can do anything which he desires to do with the police."

LaRocca was also head of the Protecto Ink Corporation, an illegal bootlegging company whose method of operation Susce could not successfully identify. "I have been told that the former janitor of this building [the American State Bank Building where the corporation was headquartered] knows the details and the workings of this corporation," he noted for the Intelligence Division.

Susce explained that LaRocca "made plenty of money" in the Protecto Ink Corporation. "One of the confidential friends of LaRocca, namely Joseph Durzo, proprietor of a gas station on Bennet St., Pittsburgh, told me that if he had the money which John LaRocca made out of illegal bootlegging in annuities, he would not have to work for one hundred years. He said he knew this to be true because he took a trip with LaRocca and his crew on one of his [bootlegging] deliveries. He told me he went with them to Buffalo, New York, to pick up a load of liquor to be brought to Pittsburgh. He told me that LaRocca receives protection from a prominent man in Pittsburgh whose name he will release only to a representative of the United States Bureau of Taxation Intelligence Division, Washington, D.C." Susce claimed that this corporation was protected by Jack Herron, minority County Commissioner of Allegheny County. The "inseparable pals" in the Protecto Ink Corporation were LaRocca, Gigliotti, Mike De Rosa, Sr., an alderman; and Mike De Rosa, Jr., an undertaker in East Liberty.

LaRocca's attorney, at this time, was Zeno Fritz, former assistant United States Attorney in western Pennsylvania, whom Susce also charged with criminal activity. Fritz, Susce pointed out, was the chairman of the Board of Directors for the Twentieth Century Towel Supply Corporation. Supposedly, Fritz had told Susce that when a racketeer needed money "all he had to do was contact some high class racketeer of the LaRocca combine, and that he, the racketeer, would receive a certain code message for a certain bank and the money would be there; but that the code would only be good for a day. Here we have a former clerk of the United States Commissioner telling a government agent how the rackets operate. This is no hearsay, these are facts."

Exhibit O of Susce's report was devoted to Patsy Meola, another partner in the LaRocca combine. Meola was arrested in 1939 for operating a lottery and freed by Magistrate Papale. "Mr. Patsy Meola never made income tax returns in his life prior to 1937 although he was making a fortune out of illegal operations as far back as 1926. He even wanted to take his own life when summoned into the Federal Building, Pittsburgh. For complete details see George Messner. Messner knows the complete history of the case and will relate same to a Treasury Agent . . . Meola was appointed a boss by Charles Papale in the respective wards mentioned and he reports only a trifling sum of $1560 for 1939 income tax purposes. He is a reputed wealthy numbers baron . . .

"In Meola's income tax return he stated he was self-employed and he received his income from the numbers. Here is a wealthy numbers man turning in his daily receipts to John LaRocca each year but reporting only $1560 for income tax purposes . . . In the calendar year 1938 he also made a fraudulent income tax return. He reported the identical net as for 1937, $1560. In this year he also turned his daily receipts into John LaRocca's combine; which latter was receiving protection from Charles Papale, the Pittsburgh City Police Inspectors, and the Pittsburgh Superintendent of Police . . . In 1939 Meola also made a fraudulent income tax return; and that year he made a tremendous lot of money with LaRocca as he was appointed head bookie in 1939 in the eleven and twelve wards . . . In 1940 Meola reported the same income as in prior years, that is $1560 . . . When the man is investigated a sizeable income should be discovered. He is concealing reputedly a tremendous fortune. See George Messner and Mike De Rosa, Jr. for complete details."

Dozens of allegations of wrongdoing, similar to those preceding, were strewn throughout Susce's report. Many of the allegations, rambling as they were, led from one person to another, connecting racketeers to city officials and vice versa. In Exhibit U, Susce wrote, "Everyone in the County of Allegheny knows that Andrew T. Park, then [1939] District Attorney, was the protector of the rackets. He fired his ace detective Peter Connors because Connors did not return his income from the rackets to Park, while Park was on a vacation tour. On one occasion Connors told the County Detectives to raid all the bawdy houses in the County but to stay away from Fay Allison's place. Fay Allison was also known as Fay Peterson. She made a fortune out of bawdy houses and at present is in Miami, Florida. She never made an income tax return in Allegheny County . . . Mr. Andrew T. Park was an associate of Sebastian LaRocca in the bootlegging days."

Early in the report, Susce had written that "the largest policyracketeer [sic] of the Pittsburgh numbers combine is Arthur Rooney the political boss of the North Side of Pittsburgh . . . This was told me by George Messner on August 16, 1943 on Liberty Ave."

In Exhibit C, where Susce disclosed information about the Twentieth Century Towel Supply Corporation and the numbers racket, he told how the numbers game was being played in Pittsburgh's Federal Building. "It is beyond human comprehension," he wrote in an outraged tone, "how the United States Government while instituting an investigation of a racketeer should allow within the walls of the Post Office a numbers concession to be operated daily. The Negro porter (shoe shine boy) goes all through the building writing numbers. This is verified by a United States Zone Deputy Collector who played a number for fifty cents and hit. This writer is a worker for the LaRocca combine." When the lucky Collector, a Mr. Travis, had told Susce about the numbers hit, he was unaware that Susce was investigating John Sebastian LaRocca.

Susce also referred to a *Bulletin Index* magazine article of 1939 which told of "newsboy Ben Lazarus [who] continues making his numbers rounds in the City County Building,

Pittsburgh . . . Ben Lazarus turns in his daily receipts to a fellow member of LaRocca's combine."

Throughout the report, Susce posed questions for the Intelligence Agents whom he hoped would prolong his investigation. He was suspicious of everyone and everything. "Why did John LaRocca use so many aliases?" "Where are the capital stock transactions of the Twentieth Century Towel Supply Corporation?" "Why did the police dismiss charges against twelve men who were arrested for racketeering?"

When the local press reported that twenty-five persons had been arrested for gambling and numbers racketeering, Susce asked, "How about their income from illegal rackets?" When the numbers bosses threatened to link names of politicians with numbers graft if the city didn't abandon its "clean up" campaign, Susce demanded, "Who are these numbersmen?"

In many instances, Susce provided leads for the follow-up investigators. "See George Messner, or Angotti, or De Rosa for details," he'd written. When twenty men were fined for racketeering, Susce suggested "The United States Investigators should contact the morgue records of the Bulletin Index to discover the identity of these men."

At every rock in his path Susce sniffed like a bloodhound for clues of criminal activity. Few clues escaped him, though many perplexed him. Those, he felt, were the clues that required closer scrutiny by the Intelligence Division.

A cursory reading of the Susce report, as this document would eventually be tagged, revealed a jumbled, sometimes incoherent tale that was barely believable. Susce's lack of expertise as investigator and his erratic prose style contributed to this lack of conviction. To the noncommitted reader, the Susce Report was a bundle of unsubstantiated charges leveled at racketeers and public officials. While the tale showed promise as a thrilling novel about Mafiosi and politicos, it was difficult to consider it factual. Therefore, its value as a government investigation seemed nonexistent; its creator without merit.

To a reader familiar with the business of organized crime, however, the Susce Report did carry conviction. It would have been possible to document many of Susce's charges. A Grand Jury investigation, for example, could have clarified much of the vagueness of the report. Less formally, the records of Pittsburgh's newspapers could have substantiated Susce's charges in many instances.

The media had not ignored the police raids of numbers spots nor had they overlooked the threats and resignations that had followed each raid. The Mob in Pittsburgh was not a secret organization. Pittsburghers had every reason to believe their city was racket-riddled. The Susce Report was provable and its findings, responsibly organized for use in a court of law, could have put the Mob out of business in the country's tenth largest city.

Responsibility for forwarding the Susce Report to the proper authorities, so that it could be acted upon, lay with Collector Granger. But by December, 1943, when Susce completed his report, the Mob in Pittsburgh, as well as across the country, was already preparing to profiteer out of post-World War II America. Money would flow then like in few other eras of American history. Homes, vacations, cars, travel trailers, gambling—all these things would be needed to satisfy the affluent, jubilant America. And the Mob, true to its character, would be geared up for the social changes. America's victory and ensuing celebration would be used to further inflate the Mob's bank rolls and power in the nation's economic and political circles.

Publicity for and action on the Susce Report would be untimely indeed. Even if John Sebastian LaRocca were an alien in the United States who controlled aldermen, policemen, mayors and other civil servants—all to the advantage of his illegal rackets and combine—so be it. John Sebastian LaRocca would protect his interests, or rather, his interests would protect the don of southwestern Pennsylvania. But not entirely without resistance from the tenacious civil servant, Andrew J. Susce.

CHAPTER FOUR

# Blowing the Whistle

On December 14, 1943, as Zone Deputy Collector Andrew J. Susce entered his bureau office on the fourth floor of Pittsburgh's Federal Building, he carried in his briefcase the 300-page document that exposed the core of Pittsburgh's most fierce and prosperous combine. There were other Mobs operating in other parts of this big industrial town, but the Sebastian LaRocca gang dominated the scene and held the tightest grip on the citizenry. If Susce had his way, LaRocca's grip would be loosened within a matter of months.

Once the officials in Washington, including J. Edgar Hoover, read Susce's Report and its exhibits, the shroud of protection surrounding LaRocca would be torn and the "king" himself would be sent to prison, or perhaps deported. Susce was sure that the numbers books provided by James Angotti and the confession of LaRocca's partner Joseph Brusco would be sufficient evidence for a Grand Jury to return true bills against the cast of characters in his report.

The books and the confession "will suffice to convince any jury," Susce had written in concluding his report, "that a flagrant violation of the United States law has been committed: namely, the income tax law of the United States. A violation of the income tax law coupled with fraud constitutes a felony. Therefore, the names of the men who are given as numbers men, pick-up men, writers and operators, all are guilty of a felony . . . This [report] should go to the United States Intelligence Division for further investigation."

Following this further investigation, leading, as he hoped, to the appropriate convictions, Susce expected to be hailed a national hero. After all, he had penetrated the LaRocca combine. He alone would be responsible for the exposure of John Sebastian LaRocca, et al. But Susce knew that if his moment of glory were ever to come, his report would have to be sent to the proper officials in Washington, D.C. He was determined to get it there, if he had to deliver a copy himself.

"John," Susce said somberly to his agent-friend John Orlasky, "I'm turning in my report today. All hell will break loose when this report hits Granger's desk."

"Andy, you're going to hang yourself," Orlasky muttered shaking his head. Orlasky was one of maybe two or three field agents to whom Susce had confided about the LaRocca investigation. Once, in fact, Orlasky had assisted Susce in obtaining some information about the combine, but he was chary of Susce's assignment.

"John, this report will blow the lid off Washington. Mr. Hoover might say there isn't a Mafia in this country, but when he reads my report he'll believe otherwise."

"Your report won't get to Washington," Orlasky predicted to his friend.

"Oh yes it will. One way or another it'll get there, John, because I have a copy of it." It was against government regulations for an agent to keep a copy of a bureau report for his personal use, but Susce had ignored the rule. He had instructed the secretary who typed his report to make a carbon copy. "This report might be too hot for some people to handle," he told Orlasky, "and I'm not going to let it be ditched."

Susce knew his superiors were anxious to receive his report. There had been constant pressure on Collector Granger and then O'Malley to find out just what, if anything, Agent Susce had uncovered. After Susce interviewed LaRocca, the don wanted to know what the government had on him.

Word of the investigation had reached Jimmy Kirk and David Lawrence, and while they would have figured that Granger had the matter under control, they nonetheless wanted the Susce Report expedited. The sooner it was in Granger's hands, the sooner it could be suppressed. Susce felt the pressure in the final weeks of his investigation when O'Malley refused his requests for assistance from a Special Agent and urged him to turn in his report.

Susce believed that O'Malley was not above destroying a report. Once during the LaRocca investigation Susce had gone to O'Malley and asked to see a tax report that he had earlier prepared on Joseph Gigliotti, the fearsome numbers boss. O'Malley told him the report had been burned after Gigliotti paid his delinquent taxes. After that, Susce felt he couldn't trust O'Malley, particularly with a report that could wipe out John Sebastian LaRocca's combine and expose the Democratic Party in Pittsburgh.

Shortly before noon on December 14, 1943, Susce walked into the office of Stanley Granger's secretary and asked to see the Collector. He wasn't in. Susce told the secretary, Clara Hoppman, that he had a report to deliver and he asked when Granger would return. The secretary didn't know, but she told Susce that she would take the report and lock it in the office safe. Susce hesitated but then decided to leave the report, in exchange for a receipt for it from Miss Hoppman. He waited and watched while his nine-month project was put into the safe.

"Why are you watching me?" Miss Hoppman asked Susce.

"I just want to make sure . . ." Susce answered politely, and left the office.

Susce never knew when Granger read the LaRocca investigation, but his boss undoubtedly read the report within hours after it was placed in his safe. Regardless of when he read it, Granger would have been shaken by its contents. The patsy he had thought the perfect choice for an investigation of John Sebastian LaRocca had turned in a scathing report. Susce had uncovered more information about the Pittsburgh Mob than any government agent in the history of the Bureau of Internal Revenue.

In spite of its deficiencies and incoherence, the report could not possibly be sent to Washington, D.C. Granger knew that if J. Edgar Hoover were to read and believe Susce's report, the FBI would descend upon the taxman's Pittsburgh office with a warrant for his own arrest. Susce's allegations would result in one of history's most shameful exposures of venality within an agency of the United States government. The allegations would also neutralize the Democratic Party in Allegheny County.

Collector Granger obviously decided to "fix" the report. He had underestimated Susce's enterprise, but thought he knew how to manipulate a Zone Deputy Collector. He would direct Susce to rewrite the report so that it was a whitewash and not a document that would destroy his own administration. For the moment, however, action on the report would be delayed until after the first of the year.

The New Year at the Bureau of Internal Revenue was never enthusiastically celebrated. The Bureau of Internal Revenue was responsible for collecting the taxes that generated the nation's wealth. The first of January was a reminder that a great deal of work would be coming along, and that this busy period would persist for the next several months. The tax season was especially unpopular among Zone Deputy Collectors for they were responsible for attending to the thousands of taxpayers who flocked to the dull offices of the Federal Building for free assistance in filing their tax returns. In Pittsburgh, as in other major metropolitan areas, branch offices were opened by the bureau to accommodate the taxpayers who lived in suburbia. For that reason, just after January 1, 1944, Andrew Susce was transferred to the bureau's field office in Wilkinsburg.

About one month after he had turned in his report, Susce was in the Wilkinsburg office when he received a telephone call from Lucille Miller, Granger's receptionist. The Collector wanted to see him the next morning. Susce had expected the call so he didn't ask the nature of the Collector's business. And he wasn't surprised the next morning when he arrived at the Federal Building and found Granger in a fury.

"Susce," the Collector yelled the moment the field agent walked into his office, "what did you do? I was a United States attorney for many years but never in my life have I seen a report like yours. Who helped you?"

"No one helped me, Mr. Granger," Susce replied.

"This is a thorough report," Granger insisted from behind his desk. "Who helped you prepare it?"

Susce guessed that Granger was fishing. "Mr. Granger," Susce said, "no one helped me. I did it all. And I want my report to go to Washington, D.C."

"Absolutely not," Granger shouted. "This report can't go to Washington in its present form. Before this report goes up I want it totally rewritten and I want all the names taken out. Why, you've accused the Democratic Party in western Pennsylvania of being a criminal organization!"

It was suddenly clear to Susce that Granger intended to bury the report. He had expected as much. But Susce would not cooperate in a whitewash and the Collector was stunned to hear him say it.

"You won't change the report?" Granger asked, leaning forward in his seat, as if he hadn't heard Susce the first time.

"No sir, I can't."

"What do you mean, you can't? I'm telling you to."

"Mr. Granger, I can't do it. It's not honest. I just can't do it," Susce said.

Granger seemed dumbfounded. For a moment he didn't know what to say. Then he appeared to relax. "All right, Susce, you go back to work. I'm going to discuss this matter with Washington and I'll get back to you."

About a month later, in mid-February, Granger summoned Susce to his office for a second visit. The meeting was shorter this time and the Collector's mood had improved. Granger told Susce that if he cooperated in rewriting the report, he would be assigned to Franklin D. Roosevelt's presidential campaign in 1944.

Susce refused the offer. He wanted to work for Roosevelt, but not this way. Granger asked Susce to think about the offer until their next meeting.

The third meeting came in mid-March, when Miss Miller called Susce and said that Granger wanted to meet him the next day. However, rather than a morning meeting, as in the case of the first two, Miss Miller told Susce the Collector expected him after five o'clock, when the offices would be closed. Susce was immediately cautious and wondered if Granger was trying to trap him.

He arrived at the office at 2:30 the next afternoon but Granger let him wait until five o'clock. Susce used his time to make his presence known. He talked with several secretaries and field agents and made a point of telling them that he was in to see Collector Granger, but that the Collector insisted upon an after-hours meeting.

Shortly after five, Susce was invited into Granger's office. The Collector, whom Susce had rarely seen in four years of employment with the bureau, but had recently seen three times in as many months, was behind his desk, his suit coat off and his white shirt sleeves rolled up to his elbows.

"Andy," Granger said as he motioned to a chair for the agent to sit in, "have you considered my offer?"

"I have, Mr. Granger, and like I said before, I can't rewrite that report. It belongs to the people of the United States. It should be sent to the Intelligence Division. Millions of dollars are escaping taxation."

The room fell silent with Granger deep in thought, twisting his swivel chair away from his visitor. He had tried to persuade Susce, but now he knew his attempts had failed. This man who sat across from him, neatly dressed in a dark suit, serious but attentive, was like few other men he had ever met.

"Susce, I'm going to give you another five minutes to think it over," Granger said. "This report," he pointed to a large brown envelope in the corner of his desk, "has to be rewritten or burned. And you're the man who has to do it."

Susce sat motionless as Granger walked out of his office and into the next room. He stared at the brown envelope which contained his report. What, he wondered, would Granger do next? The bureau was Susce's career. He had a daughter who was suffering from rheumatic fever and she needed attention. He was just recovering from the Depression, making a little more than $150 a month. He needed his job. But he'd been through this mental conflict time and time before, starting the day he had first read J. Edgar Hoover's letter. This had become a test of honor and integrity. Susce knew he would not change the report. He couldn't.

"Well?" Granger said when he returned.

"Mr. Granger, I've done exactly what the government told me to do. I told O'Malley before I started that I didn't want the assignment. You knew that. I requested Special Agents to help me before I got into this jam. You denied the help. So now you're asking me to take this home and change it or burn it?" Susce pointed to the brown envelope. "That's impossible, Mr. Granger. I can't do it. I just can't do it."

"Is that your final answer?"

"Yes, sir. It is." Susce stood up and walked to the door.

"Susce, do you have a copy of that report?"

"Mr. Granger, that's none of your business."

The next day, Susce was at his job in the Wilkinsburg office when an FBI agent came in to pay his taxes.

"What are you doin' here?" Susce ribbed the agent, whom he knew casually. "You know more about the tax laws than I do."

The FBI man didn't smile. "Andy, you don't know what I went through yesterday. I had a warrant for your arrest."

"You had what?" Susce thought he'd misunderstood.

"I was waiting for you outside the Federal Building last night on Grant Street. I was told that if you came out with a brown envelope I was to pick you up because you were stealing government property. Thank God when I saw you come out you didn't have anything in your hands."

Susce shuddered. He could have been sent to prison. At last he knew Granger's ploy. His report on John Sebastian LaRocca would never be forwarded to Washington, D.C. Susce was convinced of it.

"Thanks for the information," Susce told his friend. "I've got to do something about that."

Susce couldn't be silent about a cover-up any more than he could cooperate in a whitewash. He had learned from former Collector Driscoll that bureau agents were compelled to inform the Commissioner of the bureau whenever they had knowledge of criminal conduct in the office of their superiors. Susce decided that Joseph D. Nunan, then Commissioner, should be apprised of the situation in Pittsburgh.

That day, Susce wrote a letter to Nunan and explained that an investigation of John Sebastian LaRocca, racketeer, was being suppressed by Stanley Granger in the Pittsburgh office of the bureau. Susce also said the investigation had been ordered by J. Edgar Hoover and it revealed more than $180 million of Mob money that had escaped taxation by the United States government. Moreover, Susce said that Granger was suppressing the report to protect himself and the Democratic Party in Allegheny County.

When Susce mailed the letter to Washington, D.C., he expected Nunan to come to Pittsburgh, investigate the charges, fire Granger and order an Intelligence investigation of the LaRocca combine. But what Susce didn't know was that Nunan himself was a criminal in office and would eventually be sent to prison.

In early April, 1944, there was no word from Nunan but Susce received his bureau efficiency rating for the year ending March 31, 1944. Bureau efficiency ratings were supposedly based on merit in accordance with an employee's performance in his job. A "Very Good" rating, which carried with it a pay raise, was the highest mark an employee could obtain, while the lowest mark was considered "Fair," meaning unproductive. Employees rated "Fair" were not entitled to pay increments and they were considered probationary. In previous years, Susce had always received "Very Good" or "Good" ratings. But in 1944 he received a rating of "Fair." He had expected it; after all, Granger handed down the ratings. Just the same, Susce knew that Granger was now a step closer to firing him. His job had provided Susce with prestige and security. It frightened him, more than anything in his life, to think that he might be discharged. He was not prepared to sacrifice his career.

Susce knew that he could appeal against his efficiency rating and so, to protect himself, he contacted an attorney whom he hoped would represent him. For months, Susce had read about Harry Alan Sherman, a Pittsburgh lawyer who took on racketeers in the courtroom. He hoped that Attorney Sherman would act for him.

By June, Susce had still not heard from Nunan, nor had he had any further meetings with Granger. His guess was that the Susce Report remained locked in Granger's safe while the LaRocca combine continued to flourish and elude the United States Bureau of Internal Revenue. Susce then wrote a letter to W. H. Wolff, Chief of the Intelligence Division in Washington, D.C., asking that he, Susce, be called to Washington to discuss "a serious matter."

At about the same time that he wrote to Wolff, Susce also sent a letter to Robert W. Cory, Chief of the Intelligence Division in Pittsburgh. Susce told Cory what he had already written to Nunan: Granger was suppressing his investigation of LaRocca.

Not long thereafter, Wolff replied to Susce's letter and denied his request. "Receipt is acknowledged of your letter in which you indicate your desire to come to Washington, D.C., concerning a matter of yours. The matter is being gone into very carefully and there is no need for you to come to this city in connection therewith." Susce, though disappointed by the contents of the letter, was still hopeful. He noted the line, "The matter is being gone into very carefully . . ." Apparently, he figured, the Intelligence Division, perhaps through his letter to Nunan, had already been informed of the LaRocca investigation.

A few days later at the Wilkinsburg office, Susce took a telephone call from Robert Cory. The Intelligence Chief instructed Susce to leave his desk and go to a nearby drugstore where he should use the public telephone and call Cory's office. Susce did as he was told, baffled by the secrecy.

"Susce," Cory said over the phone, "I want you to come to my office immediately. Don't tell anyone where you're going. It's in reference to the letter that you wrote the Commissioner . . ."

Susce was suspicious of Cory's peculiar instructions and he was afraid that it was another of Granger's schemes. Against

Cory's directive, Susce told Frank Holland, his superior in Wilkinsburg, that he had been summoned to the downtown office.

The bureau's Intelligence Division had its offices on the ninth floor of the Union Trust Building in Pittsburgh. When Susce arrived, he was met by Cory and Alfred Fleming, Cory's boss who had come over from Philadelphia.

Cory began the conversation. "Andy, you sent the Commissioner a letter claiming that your report on John LaRocca was going to be destroyed. Are you sure about that? That's a serious charge."

"That's what Granger wanted me to do with the report," Susce replied.

"Mr. Granger asked you to destroy the report?"

"That's right. He said it exposes too many people"

The meeting continued for about a half hour, during which time Cory and Fleming questioned Susce about the nature of his investigation and his meetings with Granger. To back up his allegations, Susce gave Cory three handwritten notes which he had recorded following each of his meetings with Granger. The notes were Susce's recollections of what had transpired during the meetings with the Collector.

Finally, Cory told Susce that he and Fleming would visit Granger's office the next day and secure the report.

The following morning, Susce was in the Wilkinsburg office when he received a second call from Cory. Again, Susce was told to report downtown to the Intelligence Division.

When Susce walked into Cory's office the Susce Report was in Fleming's hands. "Now are you satisfied that I'm telling the truth?" Susce asked.

Cory told Susce to identify the report. It was all there, including the numbers books and Brusco's confession. "And these," Susce said holding two folders that contained papers which had not been included with the LaRocca investigation, "are reports that I filed months ago. They're also on racketeers, friends of Granger's. Why weren't these reports sent to your office?" Susce demanded of Cory.

The Intelligence Chief remained silent. He stuffed the report and exhibits back into a brown envelope. "Mr. Susce," Fleming asked, "do you have a copy of this report?"

"Any damn fool would make a copy of that report, knowing what I know," Susce replied. "I knew my report would never be sent to Washington."

"How did you know?"

"Because of the circumstances. This report on Sebastian LaRocca is too hot to handle. It exposes too many people. I had to keep a copy of it to protect myself."

Cory asked Susce to bring his copy of the report to the Intelligence office the next morning. Susce said he would not.

"We don't want to keep it," Fleming explained. "We just want to ascertain that your copy reads the same as the original. I promise you can leave with the report in your hands."

Susce agreed and the next morning brought his copy of the report to Cory's office and read it word for word while Cory followed on the original. By noon, they had agreed that Susce's copy was identical and the Zone Deputy Collector was told to return to Wilkinsburg. Before Susce left the office, however, Fleming warned him, "Mr. Susce, if you ever leave the service you'll have to surrender your copy."

Susce laughed. "I'm glad you told me that, Mr. Fleming. I'll make another copy." And he left.

The next month, in August, Susce packed his family's suitcases and boarded a bus with his wife and two children. They traveled to Ohio to visit Agnes' family. The strain of the LaRocca investigation, and the worry about Granger's reaction to it, had been shared by Susce's wife and children. They were not privy to the details of the bureau investigation, but they knew of its implications and they were frightened. A vacation might ease their anxieties.

Susce stayed with his family through late August and then

Andrew J. Susce today.

Richard L. Thornburgh, United States Attorney, Southwest Pennsylvania, in the early 1970s. He later became Assistant Attorney General of the United States.

Former Senator John J. Williams, Delaware, a fighter on Susce's behalf.

# Payoff Report st,' Senate Told

## Fired Tax Man's Charges Never Aired by U. S.

### Granger's Aides, Numbers Men Accused

International News Service

WASHINGTON, June 23. —A discharged Pittsburgh Internal Revenue agent's report accusing racketeers of payoffs to public officials and politicians was suppressed and then destroyed, it was charged in the Senate today.

The accuser—Sen. John J Williams, a Delaware Republican—said Andrew J. Susce, the agent, was fired in 1944 by Stanley Granger, then collector in Pittsburgh, for making the report.

The Senator said the report contained allegations of payoffs by underworld characters and also involved specifically the delinquent tax claim against John La Rocco, whom Williams labeled "a notorious Pittsburgh racketeer."

Williams demanded that Internal Revenue Commissioner Andrews furnish him a list of persons who might have been connected with destruction of Susce's report.

### PROBE DEMANDED

Williams put into the Senate record correspondence between Susce and tax and Civil Service officials about his discharge, as well as a story from the Pittsburgh Sun-Telegraph of Jan. 12, 1945, quoting Susce as demanding a grand jury investigation of his report.

The grand jury demand was made by Attorney Harry Alan Sherman for Susce, then of Oakland, who Granger said was "not handling his work properly."

The Sun-Telegraph story pointed out that Susce said he never was given a hearing and that no action was taken on his appeals to Civil Service boards.

Susce's petition for a grand (Continued on Page 2, Col. 2.)

Sun-Telegraph Photo.
JOHN LA ROCCO
...involved in report...

Sun-Telegraph Photo.
STANLEY GRANGER
... mentioned in charge ...

Headline story in the *Pittsburgh Sun Telegraph*, June 23, 1958.

Inscribed photograph of former President Richard M. Nixon.

GERALD R. FORD  
FIFTH DISTRICT, MICHIGAN

MICHIGAN OFFICE:  
425 CHERRY STREET SE.  
GRAND RAPIDS

## Congress of the United States
### Office of the Minority Leader
### House of Representatives
#### Washington, D.C.

December 21, 1966

Mr. Andrew J. Susce
313 Garfield Street
Newton Falls, Ohio

Dear Andy:

Thank you for your letter of December 14 including the material which you wish to have examined.

I appreciated receiving your material and will give it my most careful consideration.

Warm personal regards.

Sincerely,

*Jerry*

Gerald R. Ford, M. C.

GRF:mc

Letter to Susce from Gerald R. Ford, when he was a Michigan congressman.

Andrew Susce with his scrapbook of newspaper stories about his case.

Harry Alan Sherman, tough Pittsburgh attorney who fought the mob and represented Susce.

*Letter from the Personnel Director of the IRS to Senator Howard Metzenbaum, denying Susce's right to a review of his case.*

Internal Revenue Service     Department of the Treasury

Washington DC 20224

The Honorable Howard M. Metzenbaum
United States Senate
Washington, DC 20510

Person to Contact:
Michael A. Altieri
Telephone Number:
376-0585
Refer Reply to:
A:P
Date: 15 MAR 1978

Dear Senator Metzenbaum:

    This is in response to your communication to my office dated March 1, 1978, regarding one of your constituents, Mr. Andrew Susce. You enclosed various materials which you had received from Mr. Susce, as well as previous correspondence from this office regarding Mr. Susce's case dated February 1, 1978.

    As we indicated in our most recent correspondence, Mr. Susce is taking issue with the statement in the July 29, 1977, letter to you in which we stated that Mr. Susce made solo fraud investigations which were neither authorized by his superiors nor consistent with existing operating procedures. No information in the materials Mr. Susce forwarded, which included Mr. Malcolm Anderson's letter to him dated October 3, 1977, gives reason to cause a reversal of this conclusion. Mr. Susce was removed from the Internal Revenue Service in 1944 on the charge of making allegations against his superior officer reflecting upon his integrity, which allegations had no basis in fact. Mr. Susce exhausted his administrative appeals, In the past years, several reviews of the case have been conducted, and in every instance the reviews have sustained the merits of Mr. Susce's removal.

Sincerely,

Philip P. Russo
Acting Director, Personnel Division

Enclosures (2)
Copy of this letter
Your enclosures as requested

---

THE WHITE HOUSE

WASHINGTON

March 31, 1976

Dear Andy:

Phil Buchen has passed along to me the sad news of Agnes' passing. I was very, very sorry to learn about it and hope and trust that you are becoming reconciled to so great a loss.

Betty joins me in sending deepest sympathy. May God sustain you in this time of grief and sadness. Our thoughts and prayers are with you.

Sincerely,

Jerry Ford

Mr. Andrew J. Susce
313 Garfield Street
Newton Falls, Ohio 44444

*Letter from President Gerald R. Ford condoling Susce on the death of his wife.*

**CHARLES J. CARNEY**
MEMBER
19th DISTRICT, OHIO

COMMITTEES:
INTERSTATE AND FOREIGN COMMERCE
SMALL BUSINESS
VETERANS' AFFAIRS
CHAIRMAN, SUBCOMMITTEE ON CEMETERIES AND BURIAL BENEFITS

# Congress of the United States
## House of Representatives
### Washington, D.C. 20515

WASHINGTON OFFICE:
2235 House Office Building
Washington, D.C. 20515
Tel: 225-5261  Area Code 202

DISTRICT OFFICES:
1008 Wick Building
Youngstown, Ohio 44503
Tel: 746-8071  Area Code 216
Ext: 3345
3346

Post Office Building
201 High Street, NE., Room 17
Warren, Ohio 44481
Tel: 399-5725  Area Code 216

Post Office Building
Niles, Ohio 44446
(Part-Time Office)
Tel: 652-9079  Area Code 216

February 16, 1978

Mr. Andrew Susce
313 Garfield Street
Newton Falls, Ohio 44444

Dear Mr. Susce:

Thank you for your recent letters and enclosed <u>Tribune-Chronicle</u> article entitled, "Carter helps Slovik's widow", and <u>The Youngstown Vindicator</u> article entitled, "Fired IRS Agent's Fight for Job Now Up to Carter".

As you know, Andrew, I am very sympathetic to your problem, and I have tried to help you solve it. Since President Carter has decided to help Pvt. Eddie Slovik's widow, perhaps he will also come to your assistance. That decision is his to make.

With respect to a private relief bill for your back pay, damages and pension, it has been my policy ever since I first became a Member of Congress in November, 1970, not to introduce any private relief bills. For one thing, the House of Representatives has very strict rules regarding the introduction and consideration of such bills.

However, the Senate's rules regarding private relief bills are a little more relaxed; so, if you can get Senator Metzenbaum or Senator Glenn to get a private relief bill for you passed the Senate, I will do everything in my power to get your bill through the House of Representatives as well.

Your interest and comments on this important matter are greatly appreciated. With kindest regards and best wishes, I am

Sincerely yours,

Charles J. Carney

CHARLES J. CARNEY
CONGRESSMAN
19th Ohio District

CJC/ajd

THIS STATIONERY PRINTED ON PAPER MADE WITH RECYCLED FIBERS

Letter to Susce from Congressman Charles J. Carney of Ohio.

returned to Pittsburgh on August 29 to report for work. He planned to return to Ohio the following weekend for Agnes and the children.

When Susce reported to the Wilkinsburg office at 8 a.m. on August 29, the office was locked and a sign on the door instructed all personnel to report to the Federal Building for a review. They were to appear with their government credentials, all field assignments and any other work in progress. Susce was confused. Mass reviews were not routine in the bureau. Nonetheless, Susce rode into center city with another field agent whom he had met at the locked door.

There were twelve field agents, Susce among them, who reported to Granger's office on August 29. One at a time they were called before the "review board" which consisted of Granger, Deputy Collector Felix Vittone, who eventually would be suspected of irregularities in his office and called before a Grand Jury; and Deputy Collector Charles Massarik, Jr., later indicted for abuse of power in his office. Susce was the last to be called before this kangaroo court.

Granger smiled when Susce entered the room. "Mr. Susce, I have a resignation here for you to sign. It's on orders of the Commissioner of Internal Revenue, Joseph Nunan."

Thin and distraught from his recent anxieties Susce walked slowly toward Granger's desk. He hoped he had misunderstood Granger's words. "What did you say?"

"I have a resignation for you to sign."

Susce looked at Granger and then at Granger's two assistants. "I'd like to read it."

"No," Granger said firmly. "Just sign it."

All Susce could see was a blank sheet of paper with a line drawn at the bottom for his signature. "Can I have a copy of the resignation?" Susce asked, not believing there was one.

"No."

"You want me to sign something I can't read? You want me to sign a blank page? I'm sorry, I can't do that."

Granger ordered Susce to turn in his credientials and his work in progress folder. Susce obeyed the order but he refused to sign the resignation.

"If you won't sign the resignation," continued Granger, "then there's no need for you to remain in this office. Goodbye, Mr. Susce."

Numbed, Susce left the room. His fellow employees had already returned to their jobs in Wilkinsburg, but Susce, almost without knowing what he was doing, hopped on a streetcar and went home. His tenure as Zone Deputy Collector for the United States Bureau of Internal Revenue had come to an abrupt end. He had not resigned, but without credentials he had no authority as a public servant. He couldn't believe it. He figured Granger would intimidate him and try to fire him, but he couldn't believe that Granger had the power to dismiss him without giving him a reason or a chance to defend himself. What about his rights? His Civil Service protection? The power of the United States government, which William P. O'Malley had said would protect him, had instead destroyed his career.

At home, alone and outraged, Susce wrote a letter to the Civil Service Commission in Washington, D.C., and explained that he had been ordered to resign. He demanded that the Commission intervene on his behalf. Certainly a public servant had *some* job security—*some* protection from his spiteful superiors.

Susce also wrote to Commissioner Nunan and asked for an explanation of the day's events. He informed the Commissioner that it was impossible for him to resign while he was appealing his merit rating.

Finally, Susce wrote a letter to President Franklin D. Roosevelt and requested an investigation of the "mysterious circumstances" in the Pittsburgh tax bureau.

Nunan and Roosevelt never responded to the letters but a Civil Service representative wrote and informed Susce that resignation was a voluntary act and that unless he had submitted a resignation no one could force him to resign. The information was of little consequence. On the evening of August 29, the day of the kangaroo court, Susce had received a special delivery letter from Granger. it read:

*August 29, 1944*
*Mr. Andrew Joseph Susce, Pittsburgh, Pa.*
*Dear Sir: Confirming my communication with you this date, I submitted to you a resignation based upon the request of the Commissioner of Internal Revenue and your rejection of the same, I am now notifying you again of your discharge from this service, effective at the close of business on October 11, 1944, your last day of service being today (August 29, 1944).*

*Yours very truly*
*Stanley Granger, Collector*

The following morning, Susce boarded a bus for Ohio where he told his family the bad news. The moment Agnes saw her husband's face, she suspected that something was seriously wrong. When she heard the story of the kangaroo court, Agnes became angry, but she was also relieved at knowing Andy was out of the bureau mess. They had survived bad times before, she reminded her husband, and they would survive this misfortune. God would protect her righteous husband.

Survival was foremost in Susce's mind when he and his family returned to their home in Pittsburgh. He wasn't about to forget the Bureau of Internal Revenue. He intended to win his reinstatement and he would continue his appeal, but in the meanwhile he needed a job. There was no sense pursuing another political appointment. Susce's political friends were either retired or, like James P. Kirk, no longer able to help Andy Susce. Instead, Susce decided to look for a job in the private sector. He had a friend at the United States Employment Agency in Pittsburgh, so that was his first stop. He explained to his friend that he had been unjustly fired and that while he expected to be reinstated, he needed a job. The employment agency knew of an opening for an accountant at the H. J. Heinz Company and sent Susce for an interview. At first glance, the personnel director at H. J. Heinz told Susce that his qualifications were "just right" for the position. But then Susce was asked why he was no longer with the Bureau of Internal Revenue. Susce told the truth and the interview was cut short. No job offer was made to him.

The employment agency sent Susce to other interviews but each time, when he was asked about the bureau, the personnel director would end the conversation. "We'll be in touch, Mr. Susce." But of course they never were.

After ten days of being turned down, some days more than two or three times in an afternoon, Susce believed the government had not only fired him but had also blackballed him from further employment in the City of Pittsburgh. Jobs were available, but not for a fired employee of the United States government.

Despite the outlook, Susce was persistent. He would receive a paycheck from the government through the middle of October, but it was already late September. Pride would not allow him to be unemployed. It was acceptable to be out of work during the Depression, when so many men were out of work, but times were different now. This was 1944. " . . . People who are hungry and out of a job are the stuff of which dictatorships are made," President Roosevelt had said in his State of the Union message the January before. Andrew Susce had heard those words on his radio. He would work at any job, but he would not be unemployed.

While the employment agency continued to develop leads for Susce, he also explored his own opportunities. One morning he noticed a "help wanted" ad in the classified section of the daily newspaper. Dun and Bradstreet, the credit firm, was looking for men who were qualified to become credit reporters and salesmen. Susce went to the company's Pittsburgh office and was interviewed by Alfred Wilburn, District Manager.

Wilburn examined Susce's resume and nodded his head in approval before asking the usually fatal question, "Why are you no longer with the Bureau of Internal Revenue?" Susce told Wilburn the same story that he had told so often in the last couple of weeks. When he finished, Wilburn changed the topic of discussion.

"Mr. Susce," he said, "I notice you were married in 1930. Do you know that in 1930 this country was in the middle of a depression?"

Amused, and relieved that the interview had not been routinely terminated, Susce relaxed and expounded on the difficulties that he and Agnes had faced in 1930. ". . . But Mr. Wilburn, when I saw Agnes I fell in love immediately and I knew I was going to marry her. There was no use waiting for better times to come."

Wilburn said he was impressed by any man with the courage to marry during the Great Depression and the next morning Andrew Susce was on the payroll of Dun and Bradstreet as an investigative credit reporter. Wilburn's decision restored Susce's confidence in himself and, to a lesser extent, in his fellowman.

Dun and Bradstreet was one of the most respected private firms in the country, and it was a privilege to work for the company, but even so, Susce could not stop brooding about the Bureau of Internal Revenue and Stanley Granger and John LaRocca. The thought that he had given the government the opportunity to rid itself of scoundrels, and instead the government had ousted him, made Susce feel bitter. He would not forgive the injustice until the United States government reinstated him with full benefits and wages.

## CHAPTER FIVE

# The Battle Begins

The inefficiency of the United States Treasury Department was well exemplified on September 27, 1944. On that date Susce returned home from a day of job hunting and found a letter addressed to him from Alfred W. Fleming, Special Agent, Treasury Department. Fleming was Robert Cory's superior and together they had interviewed Susce about the charges that he had filed with Commissioner Nunan in regards to Collector Granger suppressing the investigation of John Sebastian LaRocca. Apparently, no one had informed Fleming that Susce had been fired as his letter instructed the "Zone Deputy Collector" to show cause why he should not be separated from the bureau. Fleming wrote, "[You have made] accusations against your superior officer reflecting upon his official integrity which allegations have no basis in fact."

While Susce was amused by the timing of the letter, he was astounded by its contents. Fleming had accompanied Cory to Granger's office to seize the Susce Report. "How can he now claim that my 'allegations have no basis in fact'?" Susce asked himself.

The letter deepened Susce's disenchantment with the United States government. Not only in the Pittsburgh office of the Treasury Department, he thought, but throughout the whole system, honesty was by no means the best policy. How could the United States government pretend to be righteous while its civil servants were so self-serving? And what about the people who believed that theirs was the greatest government in the world? Weren't they entitled to the truth? These were the questions that troubled Andy Susce whenever he tried justifying the government's action against him. He had no choice but to follow Fleming's instructions. Fleming was a cog in the intertwining wheels of corruption that turned within the United States Government. Susce, with his attorney, Harry Alan Sherman, planned to expose the corrupt machinery so that it could be dismantled.

Harry Alan Sherman was a gadfly in Pittsburgh long before Susce had read about him in the newspapers. He was a stout man, not very tall, with penetrating eyes. A native of Allegheny County, Sherman had studied journalism in college and he wrote forcefully for the *Pittsburgh Post and Sun*, then later for the *Sun-Telegraph* and finally he spent a year on the *Post-Gazette* while he finished law school at Pitt. By the time Sherman received his Doctor of Jurisprudence he was torn between journalism and law. He sought the advice of William Allen White, the famous Kansas editor, who told him, "Young man, as you no doubt will have to choose, out of the many charming girls you know, which one you will take as wife, you must with equal maturity choose between the Law and Journalism for your life's work, for each is a jealous mistress indeed."

Sherman chose law but he couldn't desert journalism. Eventually, he became editor of the monthly *Keystone Republican* and retained the editorship for sixteen years. His pen was often as sharp as his tongue, but his flare for dramatics was best exercised in the courtroom.

## The Battle Begins / 105

In the 1930s, Sherman resented the attempts by Communists in labor unions to lead America into revolution, atheism and international socialism, and so he challenged the Communists and their equally unpleasant union companions, the labor racketeers. Sherman believed that if the masses of workers who sought relief from growing economic and social inequities were unable to find any established party or institution to aid them, they would increasingly turn for leadership to Communists or racketeers. He feared the masses would give opportunity to revolutionaries who heeded Karl Marx's admonition that "The pathway to revolution in the United States is the Trade Union movement."

Attorney Sherman, the son of immigrant parents who looked reverently upon the United States as a land of opportunity and honor, could not keep still while the minds of America's labor force in Pittsburgh came under the influence of, to his way of thinking, unpatriotic characters. Assisted by the FBI and the United States Department of Immigration, Sherman became the St. George of Pittsburgh. He infiltrated labor unions and launched a successful campaign against Communist agents and racketeers, defeating them before their campaigns for office got off the ground. Later, he undertook the representation of seventy-seven unions, and any subversive who dared challenge the bullish attorney's views soon felt the heat.

Harry Alan Sherman was brilliant. Armed with the power of the law and a thirst for justice, he feared no man. Throughout his tough and sometimes risky battles, Sherman maintained his independence and remained a registered Republican even while the Democratic Party was the self-appointed party of labor.

Susce's case against the government was perfect for Sherman, whose offices were in Pittsburgh's Carleton House, just across the street from the William Penn Hotel. Having taken on labor racketeer Buck White and John LaRocca's personal friend, Nick Stirone, who was eventually sent to prison, Sherman was aware of the combines that terrorized Pittsburgh. He was contemptuous of the Mob?the Mafia as he thought of it—and he would enjoy nothing more than a chance to expose the spineless government agents who protected the underworld at the expense of honest civil servants like Andrew Susce.

Tired and disillusioned, Susce had approached Sherman with high hopes but empty pockets. He knew he couldn't afford the fee that attorney Sherman would normally demand, but nonetheless Susce had to appeal his bureau merit rating; and Harry Alan Sherman, from what the papers printed about him, would know exactly how to go about it. At their first meeting Susce explained to the attorney that he might not get paid for his services.

"Andy," Sherman said in his loud baritone voice, "my mother had an ideal. She came from Russia with a dream in her heart. She wanted her family to live in freedom, where there was a better life and opportunity, where streets were paved with gold. My mother had an ideal, Andy. And if someone wants to steal my Mother's ideal, I'd fight 'em for nothing. Anybody who fights God in my presence is going to have to contend with me also. I don't negotiate fees to fight for God or my country."

Susce had admired Sherman before that first meeting but suddenly he identified with him. Harry Alan Sherman, like himself, was a man of principle.

After Susce told Sherman his story, at their first meeting in the Spring of 1944, the attorney agreed to prepare Susce's appeal. "The thing that's rotten in Denmark," Sherman said, indignantly, "is the situation that allows good civil servants to wait on their bosses hand and foot, to brown nose and keep quiet, to overlook and not get involved and to let what the political boss wants to happen, happen. It's disgusting. It's immoral and something has to be done about it."

With Sherman's devotion, and his flamboyance, Susce was

positive that the hierarchy of the Bureau of Internal Revenue would review his merit rating and rule in his favor. Sherman knew that it would be a hard battle and that it would be difficult to shake the political puppets in the local bureau. He hoped that intimidation, the tactic he used best in the courtroom to unsettle White, Stirone and other racketeers, might also work in the fight for Andy Susce.

Sherman had heard of Stanley Granger prior to meeting Susce, but one afternoon the attorney decided that he would confront the city's chief tax collector. Sherman walked the few blocks that led from his office to the Federal Building and went up to the fourth floor. Unannounced, be barged into Granger's office, said that he was Andrew Susce's attorney, shoved Susce's merit rating under the Collector's chubby face and snapped, "Why did you change Susce's merit rating?"

The Collector was caught off guard. "It was my prerogative to do so," he retorted.

And so Granger admitted to *lowering* Susce's merit rating. Sherman had noticed on the original document bearing Susce's rating that there was an erasure under the word "Fair," the mark that was handed to Susce in evaluation of his work for the previous year. Sherman thought he detected the word "Good" under the "Fair," indicating that while Susce's merit might have originally been ranked "Good," or "Very Good," someone had lowered the rating. Sherman hadn't asked Granger *if* he changed the rating, he just assumed it and Granger confirmed his suspicion.

Sherman later discovered that when Granger had changed the rating he had gone against the decision of William P. O'Malley, the Deputy Collector who as Susce's superior was responsible for the evaluation of Susce's work. Years later when he was in need of legal advice, O'Malley went to Sherman and told him that Granger had intended to fire Susce, and that lowering the merit rating from "Good" to "Fair" was part of the plan for dismissing the recalcitrant agent.

When Sherman demanded to know the reasoning behind

Susce's "Fair" evaluation, he was presented a list of approximately twelve specifications. Granger charged that Susce "did not follow the instructions from the Chief Field Deputy [William P. O'Malley] with respect to completing assignments in the proper order." He also said Susce "failed to consult his superior on matters which were beyond the scope of his assignments, and instead of submitting a report to his superiors for transmittal to the Internal Revenue Agents office or to the Intelligence Unit, he attempted to pursue the case to its conclusion." Granger was also critical of the presentability of Susce's work and he also faulted Susce's productivity.

Sherman's rebuttal required more than twenty sheets of legal paper. The appeal was filed in mid-November, 1944, by which time Susce was already working for Dun and Bradstreet. Sherman challenged each of Granger's complaints.

While Granger faulted Susce for not following instructions and for failing to consult his superior on "matters which were beyond the scope of his assignments," Sherman pointed out that O'Malley had never reprimanded Susce about his work nor had he responded to Susce's request for assistance from a Special Agent during the LaRocca investigation. "He [O'Malley] deliberately refused [Susce's requests] because his political friends were involved," Sherman charged.

In defense of Susce's productivity, Sherman displayed the monthly production sheets of two Zone Deputy Collectors who had received "Good" and "Very Good" ratings but had closed fewer tax cases than had Susce. Marius Santicola, "who had a tremendous territory and had a very large account," had closed an average of twenty-one cases per month in the rating year, and collected $9,435 for the Treasury Department. His rating was "Good."

Edward Shoemaker, "who had one of the most productive territories in the city, the fourteenth ward," had closed 540 cases that year, an average of forty-five per month, and collected a total of $32,764. He was rated "Very Good."

Susce had closed 770 cases, an average of sixty-four per month, and collected $20,570. While Susce's cases yielded fewer tax dollars than Shoemaker's, Susce had closed almost as many cases as Santicola and Shoemaker combined! And they hadn't spent nine months of the rating year chasing the elusive John Sebastian LaRocca. Sherman also pointed out that while Santicola and Shoemaker had been handed warrants (from their superiors) which led them to delinquent taxpayers in their wards, Susce was not given warrants but his cases were "based on determination in his district. Other men [field agents], never left the Federal Building but their production was high and they were rated high because their superiors saw to it," Sherman continued. "If you were not a favorite of the Chief Deputy you received little consideration and your work conditions were almost unbearable." Sherman said that Susce's productivity, despite the odds against him, was above average.

The attorney also directed the review board's attention to the erasure of the merit rating. While it was not illegal for Granger to change the rating, Sherman said the Collector's motives were questionable.

Based on these facts, the attorney insisted that Susce's rating be changed from "Fair" to "Very Good" and that Susce be reinstated to his position of Zone Deputy Collector.

Although the appeal was received by the Board of Review in Washington, D.C., on November 16, 1944, Susce did not receive a "Notice of Decision" until July 11, 1945, nearly a year after his dismissal. In a nutshell, the decision was as Sherman had predicted: "The efficiency rating of 'Fair' is affirmed."

Fifteen specifications preceded the review board's decision. They included:

"Although the appellant displayed adequate skill in preparing income tax returns, testimony does not indicate that he was outstanding in doing things in proper order in all his operations and in knowing which method to use in different cases . . .

"The appellant's letter reports and warrant reports on file were so illegibly written that they could not be easily understood. The appellant takes issue with the statements of his supervisor on the ground that all of his reports were not given consideration; however, a standard requiring that all reports be readily legible is not unreasonable for adequate performance . . .

"In spite of the fact that the appellant did refer some cases to other offices of the Bureau and contacted his superiors on cases, he had a tendency to go beyond the scope of the broad phases of his own assignment in connection with his investigations . . .

"Two examples were given of the appellant's inaccuracies in filing tax returns, and in one of these cases returned for correction, an error was again made. Another example was that of an investigation case where the report submitted by the appellant was not satisfactory to the office and was reassigned for investigation before reporting to the Commissioner . . .

"The appellant injected irrelevant material into his reports to the extent that it was often difficult to draw the proper conclusions . . .

"In a number of cases the appellant failed to make collections that were effected quickly by other deputies who took the cases over. The collections were made after the end of the rating period but the cases were pending during the rating year and are, therefore, admissible as evidence . . .

"The total number of cases processed by the appellant was higher than the average, but he was given credit in some instances for cases at the time reported for assessment and again upon collection, when, according to his supervisor,

## The Battle Begins / 111

some of the collections should have been effected at the time the returns were prepared . . .

"The appellant's approach and manner of interrogation, particularly on income tax cases, were not conducive to accomplishing the best possible results . . .

"The appellant was not entirely cooperative with his supervisors because he made contacts with other offices without going through the Collector's Office . . .

"The appellant exhibited too much initiative, which could, if carried to extremes, result in a weak evaluation . . ."

Finally, in answer to Sherman's claim of an erasure, the board noted that "Changes made in element markings are of no significance since the Board is concerned only with the facts of performance and has the authority to make any changes it considers proper in the light of the evidence presented . . . Considering such matters as assurance that assignments will be carried out, devotion to duty and loyalty to the organization, the evidence as a whole indicates that the evaluation is proper."

Sherman thought that most of the review board's rationale was ludicrous and typical of the naivete that existed beyond the local bureau. Susce could not possibly get an unprejudiced review when, in fact, the reviewing board consisted of members of the Bureau of Internal Revenue who were responsible to men like Stanley Granger and Joseph D. Nunan. "How can the bureau adequately investigate itself?" Sherman wondered.

"These points," Sherman said when he read the review board's decision to Susce, "are contrived. They acknowledge, on several occasions, that we were right, that you had acted properly, but they just push that aside and go on their own. You can see that they listened to Granger and O'Malley. And it made not a damn bit of difference that Granger changed your rating. I just can't believe it."

Before Sherman had completed writing the appeal to the

review board, Susce had presented the attorney with the letter from Alfred Fleming, Special Agent. Sherman advised Susce that answering the letter would be futile, but not answering the letter might be detrimental to his case. So the lawyer drafted a second rebuttal letter for his client, this one considerably shorter than the appeal to the review board. In the letter to Fleming, Sherman outlined Susce's case from the day the field agent was first assigned the investigation of John Sebastian LaRocca, through August 29, 1944, the day of the kangaroo court.

"I beg to advise," Sherman responded for Susce, "that I have both been separated from the service and otherwise disciplined. I was arbitrarily dismissed on August 29, 1944, without previous notice, without hearing, on no charges preferred in advance to dismissal, and without any color or authority under the law." Sherman's rebuttal demanded an explanation for Susce's dismissal. "It's the Treasury Department who must show cause why Mr. Susce was fired." Fleming, however, never responded to Sherman's letter and Susce did not hear from him again.

When there appeared to be no further action in his behalf, Susce asked Sherman to take his case to court and fight it on the grounds of due process. But Sherman knew better.

"Andy, your rights haven't been violated, that's the problem."

"Whatta ya' mean my rights haven't been violated? I was a civil servant, Harry. I took a civil service test. I had the protection of the Civil Service Commission."

"Not for your job classification, you didn't," Sherman explained. "Civil rights acts don't apply to you. The man who hired you had the right to fire you and your constitutional rights were not abrogated. You've been dealt a great injustice, but it can't be fought in the courtroom. No one will hear it. Believe me, Andy, if I could get this case inside a courtroom, I'd do it."

## The Battle Begins / 113

Susce didn't understand. He had taken a civil service examination and had understood that to mean he had the protection of the Commission. But Susce was a political appointee and there was no protection for him or any of the Zone Deputy Collectors in his job classification.

"Certainly you should have had that protection in such a sensitive job," Sherman continued, explaining to his client, "but in a political classification it just wasn't there. Due process laws don't apply to civil servants, Andy. You were entitled to an administrative review, but now you've had yours. It was a secret review, and you have no idea of what went on, but you had yours." Sherman also told Susce that there was no provision within the government for his case to be considered outside the Treasury Department. "As long as they [the Treasury officials] have control over your case, Andy, you won't get anywhere, believe me. It's political."

Sherman knew the business of politics as well as any politician. "Blackmail is the currency of success in politics. If you're going to be reinstated it's going to be the result of political pressure. It's not going to come out of the Treasury Department."

Susce wanted to know what he should do next.

"I'll tell you what to do next," Sherman said emphatically. "You let me make a political issue out of this case. That's how we're going to win it."

Sherman was skilled in the political arena and he put together a campaign for his client. His first move was a headline grabber in the Pittsburgh newspapers. Sherman petitioned then United States Attorney General Francis Biddle to convene a special Federal Grand Jury to investigate Pittsburgh racketeers and public officials who were defrauding the government out of millions of dollars in income taxes. "Fired Revenue Agent Charged Numbers Graft, Special Federal Probe of Tax Evasion and Payoffs Asked," ran the page one headline in the *Pittsburgh Sun-Telegraph*. A long article, which was jumped to the inside pages, explained that "Attorney Harry Alan Sherman filed the petition as counsel for Andrew J. Susce, former Internal Revenue agent, fired by the Internal Revenue Collector Stanley Granger."

A synopsis of Susce's case was recounted in the article which also reported that "Attorney Sherman, in the petition to Attorney General Biddle, also demands appointment of a special United States attorney to conduct the grand jury investigation. He charged that because of the close political affiliations of the office of United States Attorney Charles F. Uhl with local Treasury Department officials, 'appropriate remedial action cannot be expected to insure filing of criminal information.'"

The article also quoted Collector Granger. He said that Susce had submitted a "voluminous report" to him in 1943 and that he had followed proper procedure in forwarding the report to his own superiors in Washington, and that it presumably had been acted upon. So far as Susce's discharge was concerned, Granger said the former agent was dismissed because "he was not handling his work properly." Several weeks before this article appeared, Granger had been quoted in the newspaper as saying that Susce's report was "not important."

Despite the petition and the ensuing publicity in Pittsburgh, Biddle ignored Sherman's request. "The fix is well above the heads of anyone in the local bureau," Sherman confided to his client, disappointed that his political plan had failed. "Someone in Washington doesn't want that report released, Andy. It's too explosive."

While Sherman's plan had failed to arouse any obvious interest in Washington, it had aroused interest among the racketeers in Pittsburgh. Alone, Susce could be contained, the racketeers thought, but with Sherman, Susce was a threat. Following the publicity of Sherman's petition to Biddle, Susce heard from various sources that his life was in danger.

An alderman, who had been sent to jail for accepting payoffs, told Sherman that Susce was "being measured for a coffin" and he advised the attorney to stay away from the fired field agent. "If he wants to live," the alderman advised, "he'll keep his mouth shut."

Scared, but mostly concerned for the safety of his wife and children, Susce arranged to move his family from Pittsburgh to Newton Falls, Ohio, a small village not far from the Pennsylvania border. Agnes' elderly aunt in Newton Falls needed personal care, and the family was welcome in her spacious, brick home.

Susce's children resented their father's decision to move. They were already enrolled in schools in Pittsburgh, and they appreciated the opportunities offered by a major city. Pittsburgh was on the eve of its great Renaissance and the children didn't want to leave. They had no choice in the matter, however. Newton Falls was a tiny, farm town outside crime-ridden Youngstown, Ohio. But it was a safe town, and that mattered.

Although he moved his family to Ohio, Susce himself could not leave Pittsburgh. He had to remain in the city if he wanted to work for Dun and Bradstreet where he had been promoted to salesman at a salary that was higher than he had ever dreamed possible. Most of the money, of course, was absorbed by expenses—maintaining his apartment in Pittsburgh and keeping his family in Ohio.

Susce visited his family on weekends but for the next twenty-five years, until he retired, he could not live with them. The government of the United States had robbed him of his career, Susce felt, and now the government was depriving him of a normal family-life in which he could watch his children grow up and he and his wife grow old. Not even reinstatement was worth that sacrifice, Susce thought, but he could not give up the fight.

In spite of his now lonely life, Susce was not defeated. He liked his new job. He worked with bright men at Dun and Bradstreet. Some went on to become vice-presidents and administrators. Susce was proud to work for the nation's leading credit firm, and he was loyal to it. Without his family close-by during the work week, he devoted endless hours to the company and for many years he consistently won awards as one of the top salesmen in his district. Dun and Bradstreet was aware of Susce's political predicament, but nothing was ever said to him about it. Even when Sherman grabbed headlines in the Pittsburgh newspapers there was no request, as Susce thought there might be, for him to discontinue his fight against the government.

For his own protection, however, Susce asked his attorney to stop the fight, at least temporarily. He wanted to let it rest, he told Sherman, but he would never let it die.

CHAPTER SIX

# The Senator from Delaware

Prior to the decade that began in 1950, Pittsburgh was one of the least attractive cities in America. O. Henry, the short story writer, described it as the "low-downdest" of cities and its people as "the most ignorant, ill-bred, contemptible, boorish, degraded, insulting, sordid, vile, foul-mouth, indecent, profane, drunken, dirty, mean, depraved." It was a mining town; overcrowded, unsanitary, polluted and decaying. Despite its wealthy families, like the Mellons, the Carnegies, the Heinzes and the Laughlins, the Smoky City was without a civic champion.

Pittsburgh was dying amidst its immigrant population, the very people who at the turn of the century had settled there in anticipation of happiness, wealth and longevity. For a while, in the twenties, it looked as though their dreams would be realized, but then came the thirties and the Depression and defeat. It was inevitable, perhaps. A city without champions, a corrupt municipality—Pittsburghers had prescribed their fate.

With the Second World War the big industrial town rose to

the American cause. Following the war, champions, hundreds of them in fact, arose and pledged to remake their city. The Pittsburgh Renaissance was born. At the helm of this rebirth were the city's Democratic mayor, David L. Lawrence, and one of the nation's wealthiest men and most influential Republicans, Richard King Mellon. These two men, despite their political inclinations, used power and money to transform one of the country's ugliest cities into a thriving, bustling metropolis. With time, Pittsburgh would even shake its odious nickname, the Smoky City.

Pittsburgh was not entirely "swept clean" by its Renaissance, however. The smoke was gone, but one equally ugly element remained: corruption. As obvious as the soot and smog that once clouded the city, corruption remained at home in Pittsburgh. Despite Mayor Lawrence's contention that corruption was out of date and at a minimum, organized crime, which had established partnerships with businessmen and politicians during the Depression, was increasing its efforts to acquire even more influence and wealth. The Pittsburgh Renaissance was successful as a major urban renewal project, but it was also successful as a political ploy. If Mayor Lawrence said his city was "clean," his city was clean. The Renaissance diverted attention from the existence of crime and was therefore a boost to the business of the John LaRoccas of Pittsburgh.

In the midst of the great revival, however, a Republican United States Senator from Delaware flew into Pittsburgh, landing at the city's busy new airport, and called the Mayor's bluff. There was corruption in Pittsburgh's Federal Building, at the IRS, and the Senator had come to flush it out. He was not dependent upon Pittsburgh's political machine for his votes, so he made no apologies for busting in. Instead, Senator John J. Williams gave his story to the local press and then winged it back to Washington where he told it again on the floor of the United States Senate. The Senator was not a spoilsport, though he was a shrewd Republican in a Democratic era. He was in hot pursuit of a corrupt federal agency and Pittsburgh just happened to be on his list of suspected cities. He had already been to Wilmington, to New York and to St. Louis. So there was nothing that attracted him to Pittsburgh, other than corruption in the IRS.

In 1946, John J. Williams was elected to the United States Senate and remained there for twenty-four years. He retired from public life in January, 1971, despite the fact that he could have been elected again. "When a man passes the age of seventy," the Senator explained, "he should no longer serve in the Senate. Not that he lacks the intelligence; but the energy and the drive is lacking."

The early days of Senator Williams' years in Washington were devoted to a fierce investigation of the United States Internal Revenue Service. Tipped off by a Delaware Democrat that "an organized tax fix exists in the country," Williams plunged into the pursuit of the criminals. By the time he finished, in the mid-1950s, he was responsible for sending more than a dozen IRS officials, including the Commissioner, Joseph D. Nunan, to prison. Furthermore, his probe encouraged President Harry S. Truman to re-organize the IRS and thereby remove it from the political arena.

Specifically, instead of a state's senior Senator appointing tax collectors, like Stanley Granger in Pittsburgh, Congress would play no role in such decisions. Tax collectors would be called directors and they would be appointed by the hierarchy of the IRS. While the re-organization was not entirely politics-proof, it appreciably diminished the influence that a United States senator might have over his state's IRS offices.

The Williams probe, like the Susce Report in Pittsburgh, exposed a national syndicate of organized crime that was operating with the consent of many officials in the tax collecting agency of the United States. Skulduggery in the Wilmington tax office led Senator Williams to discover that his own tax dollars were being embezzled. And then he was visited by Jesse Cooper who had served as Deputy State Auditor in Delaware and later, in 1939, joined the Internal Revenue Service and remained with the agency through 1944. As a Democrat, Cooper was elected State Treasurer in 1944 and served one four-year term.

In 1949, Cooper learned of a "highly organized tax-fixing ring involving some of the highest officials in the Internal Revenue Service—a tax-fixing ring whereby the organized racketeers and other elements of the underworld are, for a fee paid to the right people, buying immunity from criminal prosecution and settling their tax obligations for a small fraction of the amount owed." This information he relayed to Senator Williams, with the understanding that the Senator would never divulge his source of information.

At first, Senator Williams was suspicious of Cooper's fantastic story, but nonetheless he felt obliged to check it out. Cooper's information, of course, was correct and Senator Williams protected his identity until 1971, when Cooper agreed to be identified as the source. Shortly after Williams revealed Cooper's name, Cooper died of natural causes. The then former Senator approached Delaware's governor and recommended that the state recognize Cooper by naming a public building in his honor. In November, 1971, the Jesse S. Cooper Memorial, a public health building, was dedicated in Dover. John J. Williams delivered the dedication speech.

Cooper's information led Williams to more than a half dozen major cities where he exposed criminal behavior in the offices of IRS Collectors. In Indianapolis, for example, Williams investigated the tax claim against the Indianapolis Brewing Company. For the years 1944 through 1946, the company had reported an aggregate tax bill, which it had paid, of

$185,785.25. The total, however, was deficient by $812,098 according to tax bureau records. In 1949, to satisfy the debt, the Indianapolis Brewing Company offered the government a compromise payment of $4,500. It was accepted. Two years later, the company charged that it had overpaid the government in previous years and sued for $35,000. The tax bureau's chief counsel was unable to offer a defense to the suit and so a $35,000 payment was approved for the company. Senator Williams, who brought the matter to the attention of his colleagues in the Senate, was outraged by the incident. He was even more alarmed when he considered the names of the men the company had hired to represent it in the action against the government.

"This is a most interesting case," Senator Williams said in February, 1951, "when we consider that the firm employed a former Commissioner of the Internal Revenue and a former Chief Counsel of the Treasury Department, both of whom were serving the Government at the time the claims were first made."

Counsel for the Indianapolis Brewing Company was none other than Joseph D. Nunan, IRS Commissioner from 1944 through 1947, and Theron Lamar Caudle, assistant Attorney General in charge of the Tax Division. It was unlawful for any former IRS officer to act as counsel in any claim against the United States which was pending while the officer was with the Service. Nunan, who had entered private law practice after he resigned from the IRS in 1947, was granted a "special privilege" which he had requested from the IRS, to represent the Indianapolis Brewing Company. Caudle was granted the same privilege, despite the fact that he had been fired from the service. He had been indicted for conspiracy to fix a tax case.

In another case, presented on the floor of the Senate in February, 1952, Senator Williams learned that Nunan had represented Jacob (Jack) Udell who had operated a poultry processing plant in Delaware. The IRS claimed Udell owed the government $792,094 in back taxes for the years 1942 through 1945. While the Udell case had been pending when Nunan was in charge of the IRS, Senator Williams said he could find "no record of Mr. Nunan's having been granted a waiver to represent this taxpayer."

In December, 1948, the Senator explained, Udell's case was sent to the Tax Division of the Department of Justice with recommendations for criminal prosecution. At the time, the chief of the Tax Division was Caudle. Six weeks later, by which time Nunan was representing Udell, the bureau requested that the case be returned by the Department of Justice. Udell, the tax officials explained, was seriously ill and there was some question about the appropriateness of his prosecution. Udell submitted himself to a medical examination. The examining doctor found that "the outstanding feature of Mr. Udell's illness is his anxiety."

Not long thereafter, the IRS suggested to the Justice Department that criminal charges against Udell be dropped. In December, 1949, the Justice Department confirmed their "concurrence in the decision that prosecution of Jacob Udell should not in good conscience be undertaken because of the report of the precarious condition of his health." Accordingly, the case remained untouched and the $792,094 was never collected.

Following his detailed presentation of the Udell case, Senator Williams told his colleagues that "This is the sixth case handled by Mr. Nunan and his associates to which attention has been called and in each instance recommendations for criminal prosecution have been ignored and proposed taxes totaling over $3,500,000 remain uncollected."

As the Senator continued his crusade against the IRS, and Nunan, more than 170 IRS officials were fired for criminal behavior. Many of them were subsequently indicted. But the big boss himself, Joseph D. Nunan, didn't fall until 1954 when he was indicted and found guilty of failing to pay taxes on more than $100,000. Ninety thousand dollars of unexplained income went unreported by Nunan during the time that he served as IRS Commissioner. A total of $160,000 of unexplained income was uncovered between 1944 and 1950.

At Nunan's trial, bookmaker Frank Erickson reported that Nunan had won $1,800 when he bet on Harry Truman's presidential election. Erickson also testified that when he was called before the Kefauver crime committee, he paid Nunan a $1,500 fee for advice.

Nunan's defense was that $90,000 of the unreported money belonged to his wife, who had received that cash from Tammany boss Charles Murphy. He also said that he kept $100,000 in cash at home in a safe. Nonetheless, the judge who presided at Nunan's trial told the defendant that his guilt was emphasized by his failure to properly account for and pay his own taxes. "The law abiding citizens of this country who are carrying their share of the taxes gain no comfort from your dishonesty," the judge concluded. Nunan was sentenced to five years in prison.

While Senator Williams compiled evidence against Nunan, he also stalked the racketeers who had been bilking the government out of millions of dollars of tax revenue. In May of 1952, Senator Williams brought the tax cases of three Chicago racketeers, including Al Capone, to the floor of the United States Senate. Capone, in 1942, owed the government more than $119,000, but his offer to compromise for $30,000 was accepted by the Department of Justice. Ralph Capone, another of the nation's then most deadly racketeers, was delinquent by $92,914.38 for the years 1922 through 1928. His tax bill went uncollected by the IRS; but in 1952, not long after Senator Williams had spotlighted his case in the Senate,

Ralph Capone was indicted. "The net result," explained Senator Williams, "is that for the past twenty-five years the Federal Government has been financing Ralph Capone's racketeering operation to the extent of $93,000, without even collecting any interest; and today the Government is on the verge of settling the unpaid claim for an insignificant fraction of its total."

On the day he made these remarks in 1952, the Senator also revealed the case of John "Greasy Thumb" Guzik, an associate of Al Capone and the treasurer of the Capone syndicate. Guzik owed the government $892,000 but settled the claim with a compromise payment of $100,000, or about eleven cents on the dollar. At the time he made the settlement, Guzik's income totaled more than a quarter of a million dollars.

Senator Williams criticized the Treasury Department for accepting compromise offers by racketeers but he was informed by treasury officials that the nation's racketeers "do not keep books. They [the treasury officials] point out," Senator Williams said, "that racketeers and gamblers conduct the most of their operation in cash, thereby rendering it extremely difficult for the Government to prove their cases regarding their actual earnings . . . This explanation is difficult for the average taxpayer to accept, in view of the manner in which the Treasury Department forces him to render an accurate accounting of all financial transactions."

Senator Williams' probe did little to enhance his popularity among his colleagues, many of whom were better aware than he of the peculiar circumstances that existed in the nation's tax collection agency. On several occasions the Senator asked that he be granted a congressional committee to pursue the IRS but each time his request was denied. Undaunted, he continued on his own and as his investigation was publicized in the nation's press, tax collectors in Austin, Brooklyn,

Nashville, New York, San Francisco, Boston, St. Louis, and Fargo, North Dakota, were either fired or they resigned "for the best interest of the revenue service." Senator Williams, of course, preferred that the culprits be dismissed. "Resignations merely mean that these men are being placed on retirement for life in many instances," he charged.

Eventually, Senator Williams' investigation led him to Pittsburgh, where Stanley Granger was still the Collector of the IRS. Surprisingly, Williams' attention wasn't drawn to Pittsburgh via Andrew Susce's investigation of John Sebastian LaRocca, but rather by two leather-bound books that had been kept by Granger's receptionist, Lucille Miller. She was the woman who had called Susce to Granger's office for three separate conferences in the early months of 1944.

Miss Miller, an attractive, long-haired brunette, had worked in the Pittsburgh IRS office for sixteen years, ten of which were spent as Granger's receptionist. During that time, in her personal leather appointment books, Miss Miller had recorded the names of racketeers and other notorious characters who had visited Granger. "They were inexpensive books that I brought into the office myself," she explained to Senator Williams. "I kept them innocently so I could remember who was seeing whom and when. Any receptionist has to do the same thing."

The existence of the books was brought to the public's attention after IRS officials in Pittsburgh learned that Miss Miller had turned the books over to the probing Senator from Delaware. "Eight days after she gave me the books," Senator Williams explained, "Intelligence agents of the IRS learned of her cooperation and she was threatened with dismissal."

The Senator took her case to the floor of the Senate and claimed that Miss Miller was being "blackballed from future government employment as a result of her cooperation." T. Coleman Andrews, then Commissioner of IRS, told the senator that Miss Miller's civil service records were marked with a red flag, preventing her from "ever being hired by the government again." Miss Miller's job was secure, however, after Senator Williams intervened on her behalf.

The publicity that resulted from the Miller case did not go unnoticed by Andrew Susce, who at the time was happily employed as a top salesman for Dun and Bradstreet. The Miller case moved Susce to call his attorney, Harry Alan Sherman, whom he had continued to consult about his battle with the government. Sherman, coincidentally, had been contacted by Williams and the Senator wanted to know more about Andrew Susce's claim against the IRS. Sherman had written to Williams and explained that Susce was content with his job with Dun and Bradstreet and probably would not now want to get involved in Williams' probe unless, of course, he were subpoenaed. But Susce was willing to cooperate without a subpoena and when he told Sherman so, the attorney arranged a meeting between his client and the Senator. Susce hopped on a bus to Washington and Senator Williams met him in the Mayflower Hotel where they talked for several hours.

The meeting was painful for Susce. In ten years he had learned to forget. Not that the details weren't still vividly in his mind. Along with the memories, however, came the fear and the hatred that Susce had developed during his ordeal. The sleepless nights, the days when he couldn't eat, the embarrassment for his family. All of it came back to him as he talked with Senator Williams. And the more he told, the more he wanted to tell. He had waited a long time to get even with the IRS.

Susce's story came as no shock to Senator Williams, who was already convinced that the IRS was the nation's most corrupt agency. He promised Susce he'd take his story to the Senate, just as he had done with many other cases in the last few years. He thanked Susce for coming forward with the information.

On June 23, 1953, Senator Williams broke the Susce case in the Senate chambers. "Today I wish to discuss how a Treasury agent's report on a notorious Pittsburgh racketeer has 'mysteriously' disappeared from the Treasury Department's files," Williams told his colleagues, who by this time were most attentive to the revelations of the gentleman from Delaware. "The report in question was filed on December 14, 1943, by Treasury Agent Andrew J. Susce, working out of the Pittsburgh office. Allegedly it not only contained evidence of tax delinquencies on the part of John LaRocca et al., but also contained serious charges of payoffs by racketeers to many public officials.

"Not only has this report mysteriously disappeared from the Treasury files, but also the record shows that the Treasury agent who prepared the report was fired because, when the district office failed to take any action, he submitted to the top officials in Washington the charge that the Treasury officials in the Pittsburgh area were suppressing his report and requesting that he cooperate in its destruction. As the case stands today the agent has been fired, the report has disappeared, and thus far no record of any prosecution of those mentioned in the report has been found.

"In order that we may have a clear understanding of the unusual manner in which this case has been handled, I shall review the record from the beginning of the investigation."

Senator Williams then reported the chronological records of the Susce case, beginning with the April, 1943, bureau letter and continuing through the day of Susce's dismissal in August, 1944.

"The records of the Civil Service Commission in Washington show the following notation in Mr. Susce's files explaining his dismissal: 'Removal: False accusations reflecting upon the integrity of superior officer,'" explained an outraged Senator Williams.

The Senator said Susce's appeal for reinstatement had been denied by the Civil Service but he pointed to a memorandum in Susce's Civil Service file which had been addressed to a Member of Congress who had inquired about Susce's case in 1945.

"Inquiry developed that after agent declined the opportunity to resign he was removed on charges on October 16, 1944," read the memo. "The Bureau of Internal Revenue conducted their own investigation and concluded that he did not successfully refute charges which brought about the removal. These charges included allegations which Mr. Susce made against the official conduct of his superior which proved to have had no basis in fact. He also made allegations against other employees and a large number of persons whom he accused of being members of a syndicate which controlled operations of a numbers racket in the vicinity of Pittsburgh, Pa."

Senator Williams questioned why the Civil Service Commission, which was supposed to act upon Susce's appeal, delegated authority to the Treasury Department to investigate itself in reference to Susce's dismissal. "This point is significant because it represents only the beginning of the evidence which shows that throughout this entire procedure the Treasury Department had complete control over any investigation of its activities," the Senator remarked.

Senator Williams followed Susce's case through 1944, when the fired agent had contacted Harry Alan Sherman to represent him. The Senator read to his colleagues the *Pittsburgh Sun-Telegraph* article which reported Sherman's petition for a special Grand Jury to investigate "alleged income-tax evasion by racketeers, politicians and public officials in Pittsburgh and Allegheny County." He explained that the petition was ignored.

Senator Williams continued his expose for more than an hour. What seemed to concern him most was the reported destruction of what he called the Susce Report. "I recognize that if this report of Mr. Susce's involving these racketeers and certain public officials had been destroyed, it meant that there was some basis for Mr. Susce's accusations back in 1943. To determine the accuracy of this serious charge . . . I placed an inquiry with the Honorable T. Coleman Andrews, the new Commissioner of Internal Revenue, requesting a copy of the Susce Report. On April 7, 1953, I received a reply from Mr. Andrews expressing his regret that under the rules he was not permitted to furnish investigative reports to anyone outside the Bureau except as they were furnished to an authorized committee of Congress.

"I immediately called Mr. Andrews and told him that my interest in the case was not so much a desire to read the report as it was to establish the accuracy of a charge which had been given to me that the report was not even in existence, it having been destroyed during the previous administration.

"I requested that Mr. Andrews call for the report to be placed upon his desk for a personal examination over the weekend. I explained that in this manner we could definitely establish whether or not the report was in existence or had been destroyed as my informant had claimed. Later that same afternoon I received a call from Mr. Andrews confirming the fact that they were unable to locate the report anywhere in the Treasury Department's files and he said that there were strong indications that the report had been destroyed."

The Senator requested that a thorough search be conducted for the report. On May 14, 1953, he received a confirmation from Commissioner Andrews that the report was still missing. Disgusted, Senator Williams wrote the Commissioner a letter requesting "a list of every Treasury Department employee as well as any in the Department of Justice, either in the Pittsburgh or in the Washington area, who took part in this conspiracy to destroy these records. I appreciate very much your cooperating in helping to establish the responsibility for the irregular manner in which this racketeer's case has been handled," the Senator continued. "Once we can demonstrate that under the new administration the guilty parties will be exposed I am hopeful that I can persuade my informant to relate to you direct the shocking story as it was told to me."

Andrews responded immediately to the Senator's request, informing him that he'd assign someone to the task. "It may take a little time to get the information . . ." the Commissioner explained.

A month later Senator Williams had still not received the information from the Treasury Department. Andrews, the Senator charged, is handicapped in that "there are still in his department those who are more interested in protecting the past administration than they are in developing the facts. That is evidenced by a recent tendency on the part of some of these top officials to advance the explanation that the Susce Report as such, never existed, or that if it did exist, it was accidentally misfiled. I refuse to accept the explanation that a report so embarrassing as this one . . . was lost or forgotten. That explanation is particularly hard to accept in this case when we remember that the agent preparing this report was fired because he had made the charge that his superiors were trying to do that which has apparently happened; namely, destroy the records."

The possibility that the report never existed was not convincing to the Senator. He had read the Susce Report. A copy had been given to him by Susce.

"As I pointed out at the beginning of my remarks." Senator Williams continued on June 23, "what was in the report is now only secondary to what happened to the report. In the first place the statute of limitations has rendered the report practically useless so far as concerns criminal prosecution . . . but fortunately the statute of limitations cannot prevent us from exposing those who are responsible for its mishandling—nor can the statute of limitations prevent the report from being used by the Department of Justice as a background for developing a new case . . . Those responsible for what happened to the report overlooked the fact that for every crooked government employee there are thousands who are honest, even to the extent that many of them will gamble the security of their jobs to cooperate in the exposure of corruption in their department."

Following his remarks, Senator Williams was questioned by Pennsylvania's Republican Senator Edward Martin, the former Governor of Pennsylvania who had served in Harrisburg when the Susce Report was written.

"As the incident occurred in my own district," Senator Martin commented, "I am very much interested. Do I understand correctly that from an official standpoint the record [Susce Report] never has been found?"

"That is correct," responded Senator Williams.

"Did Mr. Susce's report make charges against employees of the Bureau of Internal Revenue in the Pittsburgh district?" asked Senator Martin.

"The report contains many charges. I would rather not go into specific details as to who is involved in the charges for the reason, and I think the Senator from Pennsylvania will agree with me, that I am not willing to accept an agent's report as being factual until the accused have had an opportunity to reply to the charges. Until the charges have been answered by the individuals named, I think it would be improper to publish the report. That is the reason why I am not incorporating the report in the *Congressional Record* today . . ."

Senator Martin continued his questioning. " . . . a very

formal petition, which evidently had been very carefully prepared by the attorney for Mr. Susce, was filed, asking that the charges be investigated. Has the Senator from Delaware found any record showing that any effort was made as a result of that petition?"

". . . Apparently the only conclusion we can reasonably draw is that the Department of Justice was not in the least interested in any possible law violations, or in any wrongdoing on the part of public officials, or on the part of the racketeers. The case was referred by the Department of Justice to the Treasury Department and the Treasury Department was asked to investigate itself.

"If the Treasury Department had finally decided to prosecute the case, I suppose the Department of Justice could have been informed, and perhaps it might have been persuaded to take action. However, the Bureau of Internal Revenue under Mr. Joseph D. Nunan, who has himself since been indicted on numerous counts involving similar activities, decided that it did not want to prosecute itself. The decision was made to fire the agent, which was done. That was the manner in which the case was handled. I fail to find any evidence that the Department expressed the slightest interest in the allegations contained in the report.

"The root of all this evil centers around the policy of allowing each agency to investigate itself and render its own decisions. That is a policy still in practice and one which I have been arguing to be changed for some time," concluded Senator Williams.

Senator Martin thanked his colleague for the information.

The *New York Times* was among the newspapers that chronicled Senator Williams' remarks about the Susce Report. And, of course, the Pittsburgh papers carried the Senator's expose as page one news. "Racket Payoff Report Here 'Lost,' Senate Told," was the sixty point headline that spread across the eight columns of June 23's *Pittsburgh Sun-*

*Telegraph.* In smaller print, the headline "Fired Tax Man's Charges Never Aired by U.S." ran next to an article datelined Seoul, updating General Mark W. Clark's attempt to bring about an armistice in Korea.

Photographs of John LaRocca, Stanley Granger and Senator Williams illustrated the long piece about the Susce Report. The article explained that "a discharged Pittsburgh Internal Revenue agent's report accusing racketeers of payoffs to public officials and politicians was suppressed and then destroyed." It went on to quote various passages from Senator Williams' remarks to the Senate.

On June 24, the *Pittsburgh Press* stretched a headline across its front page reading, "Senators Duff, Martin Ask Tax Probe."

"Senators Edward Martin and James H. Duff today called for a complete investigation of charges that a Pittsburgh Internal Revenue agent's report was destroyed by his superiors in Washington because it was 'too hot to handle,'" began the detailed article.

After outlining Senator Williams' comments of the day before, the article quoted long passages from both Senators Martin and Duff. "When a report is made and disappears," commented Senator Duff, who had succeeded Martin as Governor of Pennsylvania in 1947, "the disappearance raises a suspicion of crookedness and warrants the fullest investigation. It is an intolerable thing to pay tremendously high taxes and then to learn that others have been able to escape those taxes by means that are disreputable and a direct violation of the law. Senator Williams is entitled to the highest praise for this disclosure, as well as the other Internal Revenue revelations he has made."

Senator Martin told the newspaper that he was "outraged" by the "cover-up." "I always felt our Pittsburgh office of Internal Revenue was as clean as a hound's tooth. I have always felt that Mr. Granger was a good man. But I think we ought to find out if there are still any improper people in the Pittsburgh office, and here in Washington . . ."

The *Press* had also telephoned Senator Williams and he said that "a congressional investigation is the only way in which this case can be handled properly . . . The Congress has a duty to disclose to the public the names of all persons who had anything to do with the disappearance of this report."

Later that day, the *Sun-Telegraph* carried a page one article headlined "Tax Payoff Report Suppressor Known." The article said that Senator Williams "knows who destroyed the original report alleging payoffs by racketeers to public officials, according to Attorney Harry Alan Sherman. Sherman said he talked to the Delaware Republican Senator here a month ago and Williams told him: 'We in Washington know who destroyed the original Susce Report. That will be as big a scandal as the suppression of the report.'"

In the same article, the *Sun-Telegraph* quoted Granger as saying that he never tried to suppress the Susce Report. He denied that he ever called Susce into his office and told him to rewrite or destroy the report, as Senator Williams had told the Senate. Granger said that he forwarded the report to Special Agents in Washington, D.C.

"Special Agents proceeded with an investigation and I was exonerated. Now, ten years later, it comes up again," Granger said. The Collector added that in his opinion Susce never made a private investigation of LaRocca but instead picked up the substance of his report from a story in the since defunct Pittsburgh weekly magazine, the *Bulletin-Index*. "As I remember," Granger said, "Susce wanted to be one of those super-duper sleuths. This is the first time I've heard of him in ten years . . . I never made a dishonest dime out of my job with the Internal Revenue Bureau and no one can prove otherwise."

Stanley Granger was right. No one could prove that he "made a dime out of" his IRS job. Attempts were made, but the Democrats were still in control in Pittsburgh, and "no one" could get close enough to Granger. Shortly after Senator Williams' expose, Granger left the IRS.

The latest flurry of news from the nation's capital had stirred up grumblings among racketeers as well as taxmen and politicians as the drama of the Susce Report was played for several days between Pittsburgh and Washington, D.C. For ten years the Susce Report had been lost—forgotten for all practical purposes. Suddenly it was important once again and Pittsburgh's criminal elements held reason to fear the report would be disclosed.

Then, several weeks later, Senator Williams announced to his colleagues that the IRS had found the Susce Report. He read the following explanation from Commissioner Andrews:

"In the several weeks during which we carried on the search for this report, we combed a tremendous number of files here in Washington and in our Philadelphia and Pittsburgh offices, and I must say that it was nothing short of a stroke of genius on the part of one of our investigators that enabled us to find the report. Often, as in this case, it isn't easy to find out what somebody else did ten years ago.

"Without going into the details of how this investigation was conducted, I will just say that after looking through all the files in which we might reasonably have expected to find the report, one of our investigators reasoned that if the report was still in our possession, it would have to be some place where it would not ordinarily have been put.

"This reasoning bore fruit: we found it at Philadelphia in some old general files relating to personnel, without identification as to either the LaRocca case or the case against Susce."

Senator Williams explained that in a follow-up meeting

with Commissioner Andrews, the Commissioner said "a diligent effort is being made to establish all the facts surrounding the handling of the report and to check on what action, if any, was taken on the allegations in the report."

Strangely, however, neither Commissioner Andrews nor Senator Williams ever spoke publicly of the Susce Report thereafter. The Senator explained to Susce, when the fired agent called from Pittsburgh to ask about the status of his investigation, that he was not able to ascertain that Susce's allegations were fact, and so there was nothing more he could do with the report. Any further action, the Senator said, would have to come from the Treasury Department. But the Treasury Department would not respond to Susce's calls.

Nonetheless, the Senator from Delaware had aroused the curiosity of the Justice Department in Pittsburgh. The Susce Report, now ten years old, was useless as a means of setting up an indictment, but politically it was still very much alive.

## CHAPTER SEVEN

# The Grand Jury

In the early 1950s, Americans were treated to a torrent of revelations about political and social crime and corruption. John J. Williams was not the only member of Congress to bring such tales to the attention of the United States Senate. Had he been, his name and his causes might be better remembered by students of history. There were two other men in 1950 whose Senatorial probes and disclosures overshadowed the investigations of the Senator from Delaware. These were men far more influential than John J. Williams. Men with political savvy. They chose to take their political dramas beyond the Senate, to the nation, where they and their causes would achieve prominence and thereby gather public support. Unlike John J. Williams, who was called Whispering Willy because he spoke so softly, there was nothing humble about Estes Kefauver and Joseph McCarthy. These were the men of the early 1950s.

The crusade against the IRS was already a couple of years old when Senator Kefauver, in an unprecedented political ploy, conducted televised congressional hearings. He did so as the young chairman of the Special Senate Committee to Investigate Organized Crime in Interstate Commerce. Senator Kefauver's opening telecast, in May of 1950, attracted more support than the whole of Senator Williams' revelations on the floor of the Senate. Millions of people watched from their living rooms as the Senator from Tennessee and his young committeemen fired questions at the hoodlums who had moved in on America's businesses.

Senator Kefauver's committee wasn't as successful nor as long-lived as he had intended. The ensuing publicity, however, exposed Frank Costello who had been fingered as the "Prime Minister of the Underworld." Meyer Lansky was prevented from developing his illegal casinos in Florida. They would have to await a more opportune era.

Senator Kefauver's cause was pushed aside by his colleague, Joseph McCarthy, who was fighting his own version of the Communist Party in America. "There are fifty-seven card-carrying members of the Communist Party in the State Department," Senator McCarthy charged in 1950. He further said that he knew of an additional two hundred members of the Communist Party who were "shaping the policy in the State Department." So began "McCarthyism," the new rage in America. Like the Kefauver probe, "McCarthyism" was spellbinding, but unfortunately it was not so short-lived and its repercussions would be suffered for decades to come.

The political ploys of Senator Kefauver and McCarthy were hard competition for Senator Williams' revelations about the nation's tax collection agency. His comparatively quiet, non-flamboyant crusade against the IRS was not dramatic enough for the American appetite in the early 1950s.

A majority of Americans believed that corruption in a federal agency was a concern for the righteous J. Edgar Hoover and his FBI men. And they were willing to leave Mr. Hoover to his own business. But in Pittsburgh, Senator Williams' revelations were not so conveniently dismissed. There the

Senator from Delaware had aroused the interest of the public and politicians as well. Senators Martin and Duff had insisted upon a congressional probe following Senator Williams' remarks about the ditched Susce Report. The newspapers had not allowed the issue to die. Consequently, the matter was sent to the Justice Department where it could be pursued by the United States Attorney in Pittsburgh.

In the mid-1950s, Malcolm Anderson was the United States Attorney for Western Pennsylvania. Tall, thin and conservative, Anderson was a native of Pennsylvania. He had been educated at Penn State and Pitt and was admitted to the bar in 1941. Early in his career, Anderson had served as an assistant district attorney and then as assistant United States Attorney to John W. McIlvaine. When his boss was appointed to a judgeship, Anderson was appointed to fill his spot. The United States Attorney's seat was a political appointment, at the pleasure of Pennsylvania's Republican Senators Martin and Duff. Despite the fact that they were of the same party, Martin and Duff rarely agreed on patronage appointments. They had each listed ten or twelve men whom they preferred for United States Attorney and Anderson's name hadn't appeared on either list. So they compromised, after a while, and appointed Anderson.

United States Attorney Anderson was an all-business sort of guy who had no political alliances. Once, in fact, a politician called Anderson on the telephone and asked the attorney not to subpoena a friend of his before a grand jury. "I was so surprised he asked," Anderson said later, "because I had never heard of his friend. I had no intention of putting the guy before a grand jury. But the next day I sent out a subpoena and brought him in. I didn't want anyone to think the reason he wasn't in front of the grand jury was because the politician had called me up."

Anderson wasn't anyone's political boy, but he didn't have to be. He had no desire to live politically; he was only interested in a few years of public life. It would do him good, he said, to have the experience of public office prior to joining a respectable firm and practicing corporate law.

In the three years that Malcolm Anderson served as United States Attorney, through 1958, there were few quiet moments in Pittsburgh's Federal Courthouse. His most celebrated case was the conviction of Nick Stirone, the same labor racketeer who had met the muscle of Attorney Harry Alan Sherman. Stirone was sentenced to three years in prison on an extortion case that Anderson had brought against him. Stirone appealed, won a new trial, and was convicted again. The second time he was sentenced, he pulled ten years in the federal pen instead of three.

Anderson glowed when he put away Stirone, who was one of Pittsburgh's most obnoxious characters, but his most celebrated moment could have come with the deportation of Southwestern Pennsylvania's number one racketeer and gangster, John Sebastian LaRocca. Anderson was the United States Attorney who filed the deportation case against LaRocca, only to see Republican Governor Fine, on his last day in office, pardon LaRocca for one of the two felonies that was necessary to send the don back to Italy.

For a while, it had seemed that Anderson's case against the mobster would be triumphant. Under oath, LaRocca was thoroughly quizzed about his personal and business activities and the don admitted, without hesitation, that "some" of his activities had been illegal. But, in his defense, LaRocca said that he had become a "legitimate businessman."

The gangster lord testified that his coin machine business, which included pinball machines, juke boxes and slot machines, covered all of Pennsylvania from Harrisburg west. He said he received a "fifty-fifty split" of the money from the machines, half going to the owners of the businesses where the machines were installed.

Don LaRocca also explained that he was in the cement

block business with Tony Ripeppi, one-time pal of racketeer Frank Valenti. In addition, he said he and his brother operated L&G Amusement Co., which in 1948 had been listed as Pittsburgh's largest distributor of slot machines.

During his interrogation, fifty-one-year-old LaRocca, who was overweight and balding, lost his temper only once. He was asked by City Immigration Officer James B. Bannahan if it were true that he had been caught with 50,000 numbers slips in 1939, as reported by the police and the newspapers. LaRocca frowned and leaned forward in his chair. "You want it in plain American?" he shouted, "Hell no. What are you talking about?"

Under examination by his lawyer, Charles J. Margiotti, a prominent criminal attorney who had served as Pennsylvania's Attorney General under Governor Duff, LaRocca admitted that he was not a naturalized citizen of the United States. But he said that he "loved" America and that since 1939, he had been a legitimate businessman. "My present business is legitimate," he claimed. "I pay taxes just like anyone else."

One of LaRocca's businesses, it was pointed out, was in debt to the government. The North Star Cement Block Company owed the government about $30,000 in taxes, but LaRocca said that $20,000 of it had already been paid.

Regardless of how smooth LaRocca appeared, or however patriotic, the clincher in the case was that LaRocca had twice been convicted of serious crimes. It was almost certain that he would be deported. Margiotti, however, had political clout and he didn't hesitate to use it. On the day the decision was expected in the LaRocca deportation trial, Margiotti walked up to Malcolm Anderson with a wide grin. The attorney handed Anderson a pardon for one of LaRocca's felonies.

"There goes your case," Margiotti told the United States Attorney. "You need two felonies and you only got one."

Malcolm Anderson was defeated and John Sebastian

LaRocca was not bothered thereafter by the Immigration Service.

In addition to these cases against individuals, Attorney Anderson took on the United States Internal Revenue Service. Even before Senator Williams broke the news about the Susce Report, the United States Attorney's office in Pittsburgh, then led by McIlvaine, suspected the local IRS of wrongdoings. In a 1952 Grand Jury probe, Zone Deputy Collector Frederick Altmeyer was arrested and charged with shaking down a Squirrel Hill tavern owner for $3,900. Altmeyer and two companions had told the tavern owner that they'd overlook his tax violations providing that they received protection fees. When Altmeyer was sentenced to prison, he implicated his partners, Stanley J. Barczak and John S. Baysek, who were also Zone Deputy Collectors. Barczak and Baysek were subsequently convicted.

In the meantime, Agent Barczak was also nabbed for preparing a fraudulent tax return for a Pittsburgh widow and then pocketing a $358 refund. He was found guilty and sentenced to an additional five years in prison.

On the day that Barczak was sentenced, he told the court that the local IRS office was riddled with "fraud and corruption" from "top to bottom." Thus, his charges touched off a second Federal Grand Jury probe of the practices of the local IRS. By this time, Senator Williams' expose of the Susce Report had already hit the front pages in Pittsburgh, so Barczak and Susce became principal witnesses against the IRS.

Until Senator Williams' probe, Malcolm Anderson had never heard of Andrew J. Susce nor had he read the by now infamous Susce Report. But not long after the report was found in Philadelphia, it was turned over to Warren Olney III, Chief of the Justice Department's Criminal Division in Washington, D.C. Olney, in turn, sent the report to Pittsburgh with orders for Anderson to check out its authenticity.

Prior to reading the Susce Report, Attorney Anderson had

given little thought to the possibility of an organized Mob in the United States. After all, J. Edgar Hoover had consistently denied that a Mafia existed in the country and who was Malcolm Anderson to doubt the FBI chief's word? Besides, the meeting at Apalachin, which changed Hoover's stance, was still several years in the future. In the mid-1950s, Anderson thought, there was at most a network of *local* criminals. There were racketeers, many of whom had henchmen, of course, but there was no Mafia in the real sense of the word. Not in the United States. People in law enforcement, Anderson knew, had no evidence to substantiate the existence of a national Mob.

Reading the Susce Report didn't change Anderson's mind. In fact, the rambling, incoherent report did more to confuse the United States Attorney than it did to convince him that the Syndicate was at work in Pittsburgh, with its tentacles spread across the country. The Susce Report was now more than ten years old, and while Anderson recognized some of the names in the report, like Stirone and LaRocca, he granted little credence to its broad conclusions. Even so, Anderson believed Susce's information might have made several local tax cases against IRS officials, racketeers and police officials, so he did not entirely disregard the report.

Anderson called Susce to his office to discuss the report. During their meeting, the attorney compared Susce's copy of the report to the one the government had turned up in Philadelphia. He was satisfied that they were identical and he told Susce that his report, while inconclusive, was commendable for the background information that it provided.

"It's unfortunate that this information wasn't put to use when it was fresh," Anderson told the fired agent.

"It was too hot to handle," Susce explained. "There were too many politicians who would have been exposed if this report would have been released. That's why they ditched it in Philadelphia."

By the end of their meeting, Anderson had come to the

conclusion that Susce had been an "average" employee who was conscientious and competent as a Zone Deputy Collector but not qualified as an investigator. He also suspected that Susce had been stretching the volatility of his report, but he agreed that the former Zone Deputy Collector had been purposely given an assignment that was beyond his capability.

"This thing [the LaRocca investigation] was a hot potato," Anderson later speculated, "and when the letter came down from Hoover to investigate, they [Granger and O'Malley] didn't assign it to a Special Agent, which is how you usually assign fraud cases. I think they said to themselves, 'Who can we give this to who will mess it up and so ensure that it will never amount to anything?' And they picked poor Andy Susce."

While Anderson believed that the Susce Report was useless as evidence in a courtroom, he did want to do something about Susce's plea for help. And he was curious about whether Susce had indeed penetrated the Mob in Pennsylvania. But most of all, the United States Attorney wanted to find out who was responsible for suppressing the report, and to see if those responsible could be punished for their crime.

Not long after his meeting with Susce, Anderson received permission from Olney to send the Susce Report to the Federal Grand Jury that had already been convened to look into the charges made by convicted agent, Stanley Barczak. Susce was then subpoenaed and he testified for several hours one morning about his report and the circumstances surrounding his sudden dismissal. He told the Grand Jury that he conducted the investigation of John Sebastian LaRocca on orders from J. Edgar Hoover, and said that after he turned in his report, he was told by Collector Stanley Granger to "rewrite the report or burn it" because it exposed too many people, including politicians and policemen.

Granger was then called before the Grand Jury to answer Susce's charges. By this time, Granger had lost his IRS job in the political shake-up that was ordered by President Truman and later enforced by President Eisenhower. In 1952, Granger accepted a job with the State of Pennsylvania, in a legal capacity, and he moonlighted as a tax consultant. Several of his IRS subordinates had already been sent to prison and two others were about to be indicted so Granger was scared of the Grand Jury probe, particularly one that focused on the Susce Report.

On the day that he testified, Granger told the jurors that the Susce Report, as far as he knew, had been sent to the Intelligence Division of the IRS (via Alfred Fleming) for follow-up investigation. Later in his testimony, Granger discredited Susce and said that the Susce Report was not "important." He denied ever telling Susce to "rewrite the report or burn it." Furthermore, Granger explained that Susce was fired "because he was not handling his work properly." Up to this time, Susce had understood that he had been fired for insubordination, that is, for making "false accusations against his superior officer."

Anderson was not satisified with Granger's testimony and so, in a final attempt to clarify the mysterious circumstances of the Susce Report, he subpoenaed IRS Commissioner T. Coleman Andrews.

The Commissioner had submitted his resignation from the IRS, but when he heard that he had been subpoenaed in Pittsburgh, he withdrew his letter of resignation. Anderson was immediately summoned to Washington by Attorney General Brownell who explained that the Eisenhower Administration wanted the Commissioner out of office. Andrews was embarrassing the administration by refusing to collect certain taxes levied against gamblers. Following the Kefauver crime investigations, a law had been passed (which was later declared unconstitutional) that required gamblers to buy a $50 tax stamp. Of course, gamblers who bought the tax stamp would also be arrested so they avoided doing so. Andrews announced publicly that he was not in the business of catching gamblers and he refused to order his agents to collect the special tax.

Brownell suggested that in place of Andrews, Anderson should subpoena Assistant Commissioner O. Gordon Delk. Anderson, amused by the fuss that he had created in Washington, accepted the Attorney General's advice and soon thereafter Delk appeared before the Pittsburgh Grand Jury.

Delk admitted that he was not very knowledgeable about the Susce Report. After all, it had been written and buried before he was assistant commissioner. He did, however, inform the Grand Jury that the Susce Report had never been considered for action by the IRS Intelligence Division.

When Delk heard the details of Susce's case he offered to assist Anderson's probe by ordering a Task Force of tax investigators to conduct a follow-up investigation of the Susce Report. The Task Force was given office space in Pittsburgh and for several weeks it took the names that had appeared in the Susce Report and attempted to build a case around them.

For the most part, it was a senseless assignment by reason of the statute of limitations. Many of the individuals in the report had died or moved to other cities. The Task Force failed to build a case, but it did confirm Anderson's opinion that had the report been followed up by an Intelligence team in 1944, several local tax cases could have been brought against IRS officials, racketeers and police officials. The Task Force did not report that a case could have been made against John Sebastian LaRocca.

Anderson next wondered why the Susce Report had not been acted upon by the Intelligence Division if, as Granger had claimed, the report had been sent to that division. The United States Attorney then subpoenaed Robert W. Cory, Chief of the Intelligence Division in Pittsburgh at the time the Susce Report was written. Cory had taken an early retirement from the IRS to assist the government of Guam in organizing its own tax agency.

Cory was grilled under oath for several hours in front of a Grand Jury, but he failed to remember any justifiable reason for the Susce Report not having being investigated by his unit. Apparently, after it had been taken from Granger's office safe, Special Agent Fleming had carried the Susce Report to Philadelphia and "filed" it.

While it was true that Susce's case had created public clamor in Pittsburgh in the early 1950s, the clamor subsided after the case went to the Grand Jury. The sentiment, perhaps, was that a federal probe was all that was necessary to solve the matter. At any rate, the federal probe was not dramatic enough to compete with the events that captured the public's attention in the fall of 1955. There was the World Series between the Dodgers and the Yankees. And then President Eisenhower suffered a heart attack and the nation followed the news of his condition for several weeks. As they had done in previous moments of national urgency, Americans united until the newspapers reported, "Ike At Control Again." By then, the Susce Report was old news.

In September of 1955, just a few weeks before the Grand Jury's statutory life expired, indictments were handed down against two IRS officials whose criminal behavior had been exposed by Stanley Barczak. Charles F. Massarik, Jr., head of the Audit Division and a member of Granger's kangaroo court, and William I. Dolan, Jr., Deputy Collector, were indicted for violating the Hatch Act, which forbade solicitation of campaign funds by federal employees.

Following the testimony surrounding the Susce Report, the Grand Jury sought to make a presentment. A presentment, however, was not the same as an indictment and Anderson considered it a public statement in which a person was accused of a crime but given no opportunity to show that he was innocent. "It's a dirty thing to do," said the United States Attorney, and he vetoed any action by the Grand Jury in regards to the Susce Report.

Susce suspected that the Grand Jury's presentment was halted by the intervention of President Eisenhower, but Anderson reaffirmed his defiance of political muscle and told Susce that the testimony in his case was inconclusive and he couldn't risk filing charges against Cory, Granger or Fleming.

Susce pushed Anderson about the matter of his reinstatement but the United States Attorney said, "There's nothing that I can do for you, Andy. I'm sorry." He told Susce that the United States Attorney's office had no authority over the findings of the IRS or the Civil Service Commission.

Years later, it was learned that Anderson's Grand Jury was not entirely ineffective. While it had failed to assist Susce the Grand Jury's probe had forced changes within the tax collection agency. As Senator Williams had suggested, the routine of allowing a division head to investigate his own office was discontinued. Before the mid-1950s, suspected wrongdoings within the IRS were often investigated by the very persons responsible for the crimes. In Susce's time, Cory, who was head of the Intelligence Division, was also in charge of internal security. He, of course, reported to Collector Granger. In effect, Granger was overseeing any criminal investigation of his own office.

The IRS eventually adopted a rule whereby a special force of investigators conducted internal security probes, and rather than report to a Collector, the special force presented its findings to a district field officer.

Following the 1955 Grand Jury investigation, Attorney Anderson did not let up on the IRS. He continued to pursue Barczak's charges, and before he left office in 1958 he made several additional public criticisms of the local IRS, but there were no further indictments.

About a year later in the fall of 1956, Anderson said that a number of Pittsburgh racketeers had escaped prosecution in the early 1950s for fraudulent tax returns because of irregularities in the Pittsburgh office. He refused, however, to name the racketeers or the IRS personnel who might have been responsible for the irregularities.

In 1958, Warren Olney III resigned as Chief of the Justice Department's Criminal Division and Malcolm Anderson was tapped to fill his spot. In Pittsburgh, Anderson was succeeded by Hubert I. Teitelbaum, who had been an assistant United States Attorney.

Teitelbaum was immediately involved in a Federal Grand Jury probe of corruption in Pittsburgh's police circles, a matter that had been introduced in 1944 by Andrew Susce. The Susce Report was used for background information in the Teitelbaum probe, as the report was now filed in the United States Attorney's office, but Susce was not called upon to testify.

While he had originally hoped that Anderson would clear his name, following up on the campaigns of Harry Alan Sherman and Senator John J. Williams, Susce was despondent by the time of Teitelbaum's investigation. He had begun to believe that justice was not possible for Andy Susce. The Susce Report was too explosive, the "fix" was too potent, and there was no one left to challenge the government of the United States.

## CHAPTER EIGHT

# The Champion

In the final years of the fifties, and through most of the sixties, Andrew Susce searched for a champion to lead his fight for reinstatment at the IRS. Unless he hired an attorney, which he was not financially prepared to do, Susce knew his champion would most likely come from among the politicians who served outside the State of Pennsylvania

Malcolm Anderson and Hubert Teitelbaum had not been willing to expend any more energy on his case. Nor had Senators Martin and Duff, who were now more concerned about retirement than honest government. Even an outsider, though, like John J. Williams of Delaware, would have to be unusual and non-vulnerable to take on Susce's fight. Williams was scared off, Susce had heard from Harry Alan Sherman, when the IRS went after his business interests in Delaware. Sherman hadn't been scared off, but an IRS agent had audited his records one afternoon in the Carleton House.

"There's nothing here to report," exclaimed the young field collector, a Mr. Kennedy. "You're clean."

"Are you surprised?" asked Sherman tartly. "Did you expect to find something?"

"I was told to *bring something back*," said the taxman, "but you're clean."

Sherman told Susce that his reinstatement hinged upon strong public opinion. "You'll have to get the public behind you, Andy, or those misfits in Washington won't budge." However, Sherman was committed to his underground investigations for the FBI, and he was no longer in a position actively to campaign for Andy Susce. But he offered to cooperate with anyone who was willing to fight the case.

Finding "anyone"—politician or attorney—with the moxie to fight the Government of the United States in a case such as his was an almost insurmountable task. In spite of that, Susce was determined to resurrect his campaign.

In June of 1958, Susce read that United States Senator John L. McClellan was inquiring about John Sebastian LaRocca's aborted deportation case. Immediately, Susce solicited the aid of Harry Alan Sherman and wrote a letter to the Senator from Arkansas.

> *You may not realize it as of now, but John "The Rock" is bigger than the Senate and the law, as he has proved for the last quarter century [Susce wrote from Sherman's dictation]. Of course, your former colleague, United States Senator James H. Duff of Pennsylvania, and his former Attorney General during Duff's governorship of our state, the late Charles J. Margiotti, were LaRocca's principal tools for thwarting justice. Today, it appears that he must rely upon the international crime and dope syndicate which has purchased so many public officials in the past, and has netted him honors rather than incarceration . . .*

Susce outlined his investigation of the Pittsburgh racketeer and his subsequent firing by the Internal Revenue Service. "*I was discharged . . . [by] the now disgraced and convicted Jospeh P. Noonan* [sic], *former Commissioner of Internal Revenue.*"

Susce warned the Senator,

*There is little likelihood that you will do more than perhaps stub your senatorial toes against "The Rock." You might, through senatorial courtesy, obtain some information from Senator John J. Williams of Delaware, who succeeded only to the point of spreading the facts surrounding the Susce Report and its disappearance from the official files of the Treasury Department until the Statute of Limitations afforded "The Rock" and his detestable cohorts a backdoor escapte [sic] from the consequences of the law that is being applied to citizens engaged in more legitimate pursuits.*

*I am prepared at any time to bring with me factual evidence to back up and to expand any of the charges implicit in this letter. I wonder how many calls and how many "big" people have already suggested to you that your proposed inquiry should be dropped. I wonder, too, how a government which sends troops into Arkansas to enforce integration is so completely unmoved that they will not even send a Marshal with sufficient holding power to enforce the criminal laws and statutes against such vicious and destructive aliens as "The Rock."*

Despite its forceful nature, the letter was never acknowledged.

Undaunted, Susce continued his search into the 1960s, the Kennedy years. "Ask not what your country can do for you, but what you can do for your country," John F. Kennedy told his countrymen. Every time Susce read or heard that quote, he felt bitter. The words, he thought, were an insult to him personally, as though President Kennedy were speaking directly to Andy Susce.

Not long after John F. Kennedy's inauguration as the thirty-fifth president of the United States, Susce wrote him a letter. The fired agent had earlier written to President Eisenhower, after he had been inaugurated, and before him, to President Truman. Of course, he had written a dozen letters to his hero, President Franklin Delano Roosevelt.

President Kennedy's response was short and signed by an aide. "I am writing to acknowledge your recent letter to the President. Thank you." It was always the same response from the White House, almost word for word. Their politics may have been different, but these Presidents all sounded the same to Andy Susce. He had become accustomed to their cold, polite acknowledgments.

In 1960, Susce listened as President Kennedy's brother, Robert, who was then Attorney General, announced a concerted crackdown on organized crime in the United States. At last, J. Edgar Hoover had admitted there was a national Syndicate or Mob in the United States. Hoover preferred to call it La Cosa Nostra—anything but the Mafia, which he had denied for so many years.

Robert Kennedy was the first Attorney General in the forty-year history of racketeering in the United States to initiate legislation aimed at the Mob. He was responsible for the passage of the Travel Acts, which made it illegal to use telephones, mail or interstate travel in the enterprises of racketeering. This was the first major breakthrough in the United States' war on crime. Kennedy organized strike forces—units of government investigators which included tax agents and FBI men—and mounted them across the country in cities where organized crime was most threatening.

In Pittsburgh in 1962, Attorney General Kennedy's men were after the Mannarino gang which operated in New Kensington in the northeast section of the city. News of that probe aroused Susce's interest and he thought the Attorney General should know that the Mannarino boys were associates of John Sebastian LaRocca and that they could be tied to the Susce Report.

Susce's letter to Attorney General Kennedy in August, 1962, received this response:

*"Dear Mr. Susce: The Attorney General has asked me to reply to your letter of August 15 and to advise you that the contents of your letter have been noted. Thank you for your interest in writing the Attorney General."* The letter was signed by William G. Hundley, Chief, Organized Crime and Racketeering.

Apparently, Kennedy was not interested in the Susce Report, and Susce's search for a champion continued in vain. He surmised that as long as a Democrat sat in the White House, his case would be ignored. The Susce Report, he thought, remained an embarrassment to the Democrats, for theirs had been the party in control in the 1940s, when John Sebastian LaRocca had grown to power in Pittsburgh.

Politicians, however, could force the government to reopen his case and clear his name, Susce decided, so he turned his attention to the Republican Party, at the grassroots level, in Trumbull County. From there, he thought, he'd work his way to the top men in the GOP.

In 1962, Susce entered the primary election for the nineteenth district Congressional seat in Ohio. He was living in Pittsburgh at the time, but he was a registered voter in Ohio so he ran for office from the Buckeye State. His campaign, unfortunately, was sporadic, mostly conducted on weekends when he lived with his family in Newton Falls. Unsurprisingly, he lost the primary. Later, in 1968 and again in 1972, he ran for Clerk of Courts on the Republican ticket in Trumbull County. He won both primaries but lost the general elections as Trumbull County was a Democratic stronghold.

By 1965, when Lyndon Johnson was elected President, Susce decided to await a Republican administration in the White House, hoping, of course, that the Republicans would be more sympathetic to his cause. The Viet Nam war provided too much competition for him to garner any support, politically or publicly, so he wouldn't try. He was now fifty-eight years old and tired. To everyone else, with the exception of his wife, Agnes, Susce's case was hopeless. There were moments, naturally, when Susce doubted the success of his campaign, but he could not forsake it. To do so would be to lose faith in the United States Government. For the next few years, though, while the Democrats ran the country, Susce let his campaign rest once again. He would write a letter now and then—to President Johnson and his cabinet members—just to keep his name alive, but for the most part, his energies were devoted to the Republican cause in Trumbull County and his job at Dun and Bradstreet.

In May, 1966, Susce wrote a letter to Herbert Brownell, the former Attorney General, who was with the New York law firm, Lord, Day & Lord. Susce asked Brownell to represent him in his actions against the government.

*"I note from your letter that the matter to which you refer,"* Brownell responded, *"was under investigation in the Department of Justice during the time that I was Attorney General. Even though I do not have any personal knowledge of the facts of the case, I have decided that I should not accept any case which was active in the Department while I was heading the Department and, accordingly, I am unable to represent you in this matter."*

Another letter in the fall of 1966—just to keep his name alive—went to Senator John J. Williams of Delaware. The Senator, however, was no longer interested in fighting the Internal Revenue Service. Having sparked the Senate Rules Committee's investigation of Robert G. "Bobby" Baker, former secretary to the Democratic majority of the Senate, Senator Williams, the "Conscience of the Senate," had moved on to matters of more contemporary interest.

On several occasions during Senator Williams' investigation in the early 1950s, Susce had corresponded with a minor Congressman from Michigan, Gerald R. Ford. In December,

1966, Ford was the Minority Leader of the House of Representatives and Susce contacted him to renew his acquaintance and to present him with the latest developments in his campaign for vindication.

"*I appreciated receiving your material and will give it my most careful consideration,*" Ford responded. He signed his letter, "*Warm personal regards, Gerry.*"

A year after he had written to Ford, Susce wrote a letter to United States Senator Frank J. Lausche, and asked him to intervene for him at the IRS. The letter prompted the Ohio Senator to write the Attorney General, who was then Ramsey Clark.

Clark's response to Lausche, which was signed by his assistant, Fred M. Vinson, Jr., said, "*. . . we are thoroughly familiar with the case of Mr. Andrew Susce and have examined it on numerous occasions. Mr. Susce was dismissed in 1944 because of misfeasance, and we are convinced that no violation of his rights has occurred.*"

When he wrote to Senator Lausche, in December, 1967, Susce sent a copy of his letter to another Ohioan, United States Congressman Robert E. Sweeney.

"*I have the correspondence which you forwarded and I am returning same herewith,*" Sweeney replied.

"*A review of the file convinces me that there is one essential point involved and that is whether or not there is any reasonable basis upon which the Treasury Department concluded that you were guilty of making false accusations reflecting upon the integrity of your superior officer and other employees of the Treasury Department. This is simply a question of fact that can be determined on the basis of evidence and testimony adduced at a fair trial. I am at somewhat of a position of disability in attempting to reconstruct a matter that was reviewed originally some twenty-one years ago. However, I can certainly join with Senator Williams in the observation that it seems elementary and fundamentally wrong for the United States Treasury Department to be undertaking any investigation of the Treasury Department and I see no reason why the United States Civil Service Commission could not have investigated this subject independently in an effort to secure an impartial and fair adjudication of the facts."*

Sweeney urged Susce to "immediately communicate with a competent, responsible attorney" and file a petition for damages in the Federal District Court. The Congressman pointed out, however, that "the lapse of time between your dismissal and the commencement of such a federal action will operate against you."

After consulting Attorney Sherman, Susce decided not to follow the Congressman's advice to file a petition for damages in the Federal Court. For legal and financial reasons, Sherman advised against it. He said the case would never be accepted in a Federal District Court. And Susce couldn't afford the services of an attorney for a case of so dubious an outcome. Susce agreed. The United States Government, he said, had already cost him a job and his homelife. He would not allow it to rob him of his financial security.

Perhaps Senator Lausche and Congressman Sweeney were ineffective within the Attorney General's office, so Susce penned another letter, this one to Robert F. Kennedy, who was now a United States Senator and a hopeful Presidential nominee.

*"Thank you for your recent letter requesting my assistance,"* Senator Kennedy wrote Susce in February, 1968. *"I have asked that I be furnished with a report on this matter and I will be in touch with you again as soon as I have received this report. With best wishes . . . Robert F. Kennedy."*

The following month, Kennedy sent a second letter to Susce. *"Enclosed is a copy of a letter which I received in response to the inquiry I made on your behalf. I hope the infor-*

*mation contained therein will help to clarify the situation you called to my attention. I regret that it is not more favorable. If I can be of any assistance to you in the future, please do not hesitate to let me know."* Again, the letter was signed, *Robert F. Kennedy.*

Despite the fact that Senator Kennedy had served as Attorney General in the early 1960s, he was not any more influential within the Attorney General's office than the Gentlemen from Ohio. The enclosure that the New York Senator referred to was a letter from Fred M. Vinson, Jr., Assistant Attorney General. Basically, Vinson relayed the same message to Senator Kennedy that he had a few months before sent to Senator Lausche. *"We are quite familiar with Mr. Susce and have examined the merits of his allegations on a number of occasions. He was formerly employed as an agent of the Internal Revenue Service but was dismissed in 1944 because of misfeasance. Since that time he has written numerous letters to the Department and to various public officials asserting that his rights have been violated, but our reviews of the matter reveal no basis for such a claim."*

Susce fired a follow-up letter to Senator Kennedy, explaining that if his rights had not been violated then at least he had been used by the Internal Revenue Service and therefore he was entitled to recognition and compensation for his honorable performance as a Zone Deputy Collector. Unfortunately, a bullet struck down the Senator before he could respond to Susce's letter.

While 1967 ended inauspiciously, 1968 was a breakthrough year for Susce. Richard M. Nixon was making another bid for the White House and in Trumbull County Nixon had a staunch supporter in Andrew Susce. He scouted the local newspapers for articles about the GOP and whenever a favorable item appeared he mailed it to the Nixon for President Committee, headquartered in New York City.

Nixon's campaign manager was John N. Mitchell, who later

became Nixon's Attorney General and was sent to prison for his role in the Watergate scandal. In 1968, Mitchell addressed two separate letters to Susce to thank him for his "concern for the Republican cause."

In August, Mitchell wrote:

*"We appreciate, and I know that Dick Nixon does, too, your fine support and interest in assisting in his campaign for the Presidency.*

*"I have requested that a photo and a copy of his acceptance speech are sent to you, and the same should be arriving shortly.*

*"With many thanks and very best wishes, I am . . . John N. Mitchell."*

Several days later, just as Mitchell had indicated, there arrived in Susce's mailbox an eight by ten, black and white photograph of Richard M. Nixon, awkwardly slouched in a leather arm-chair. In the margin of the photograph, Nixon, or someone, had scribbled, *"To Andrew Susce, With Best Wishes, Richard M. Nixon."*

In October of 1968, just a month before the general election in which Nixon was sent to Washington, D.C., as President of the United States, Mitchell sent this note:

*"Thank you very much for your kind letter and the enclosed [newspaper] clippings.*

*"Your encouraging thoughts regarding the outcome of the campaign are very much appreciated, as is your faithful interest and support for Dick Nixon.*

*"Thanking you and with kindest regards, I am . . . John N. Mitchell."*

Following the election, Susce thought his good deeds for the "Republican cause" deserved more than a publicity photograph of the President and a couple of congratulatory letters from Mitchell. Susce wanted a job in the Nixon Administration and so he wrote to the President and requested that he be granted an interview for employment.

A response followed from the Office of the President-Elect, Richard M. Nixon, Washington, D.C., dated December 19, 1968. It read:

*"Dear Mr. Susce: President-Elect Nixon wants you to know he appreciates your interest in serving the new Administration. Information concerning you has been received by this Office which is conducting his search for qualified personnel.*

*"Mr. Nixon has asked me to assure you that your interest in the new Administration will receive careful consideration as positions are filled."* The letter was signed by Harry S. Flemming, Office of the President-Elect.

Susce believed he would be considered for a spot in the Nixon Administration, but he was naive; not understanding that hundreds of similar letters had been sent to other applicants. And, of course, Flemming did not explain the nature of the "information" that his office had received about Susce. Regardless of what Susce believed, he was never considered for employment by the Nixon Administration and he never again heard from Flemming.

While 1968 was the breakthrough year for Susce, 1969 promised even greater rewards. That was the year Susce retired from Dun and Bradstreet; the year that he had awaited. A Republican was in the White House, and not just any Republican, but Richard M. Nixon, a man whom Susce had helped elect and a politician who personally knew the facts of Susce's case. Now the political arena was set for Andy Susce to revive his personal drama, and he was prepped for a grand entrance.

Conveniently, the stage was set in Pittsburgh where President Nixon appointed a young, eager United States Attorney. He was Richard L. Thornburgh, a Squirrel Hill native, who craved a taste of political life. Susce saw Thornburgh as his new champion.

When President Nixon appointed Richard L. Thornburgh to the United States Attorney's seat in Western Pennsylvania, the sweat began to trickle off the brows of venal civil servants in Pittsburgh. Even the area's racketeers, gangsters and hoods looked up from their nests of vice and corruption when Richard L. Thornburgh took his seat in the Federal Building. At thirty-seven years of age, Thornburgh was one of the youngest United States Attorneys in the country, and he was the bright spot on Pennsylvania's Republican political horizon.

Thornburgh was a graduate of Yale, and also Pitt, where he had edited the *Law Review*. The young attorney was in private practice in Pittsburgh from 1957 until he was appointed to the United States Attorney's seat in 1969. By that time, he had already argued cases before the Pennsylvania Supreme Court and the United States Supreme Court, and he was a scrapper—conservative but tough—tough to beat in the courtroom.

He lost a 1966 bid for the United States Congress—he ran as a Republican from Pittsburgh's inner city district—but in 1967 he was elected a delegate to Pennsylvania's Constitutional Convention, where he concentrated on efforts to reform the judicial system and strengthen local government.

His political assignments, coupled with his active civic schedule—he was a board member for the Urban League and the Pittsburgh Branch of the American Civil Liberties Union—helped bring Thornburgh to the attention of Richard Nixon's people. His appointment as United States Attorney was the best gift President Nixon could bestow upon sleepy Western Pennsylvania.

When Thornburgh assumed office in 1969, he was not aware of the grip that organized crime held on businesses and other organizations in the City of Pittsburgh and surrounding counties. But after a few months of studying his case files and meeting with law enforcement officials and crime investigators, Thornburgh announced, "My number one priority is to put the heat on organized crime in Western Pennsylvania."

And then he began. Within three years Thornburgh penetrated the Mob in Western Pennsylvania and it was a miracle that he survived. When he took office, Thornburgh inherited a staff of nine Assistant Attorneys, but within a matter of months he beefed up that number to eighteen assistants. Then, he persuaded Attorney General John N. Mitchell to dispatch a Special Anti-Crime Strike Force to Western Pennsylvania. Concurrently, he won the right to empanel a Federal Grand Jury to investigate organized crime in his district. The Grand Jury, the first of its kind in the nation, was empaneled for three years!

Later, Thornburgh successfully empaneled two additional Grand Juries—one to assist his original Grand Jury and another to attack the narcotics problem in Western Pennsylvania.

Within a few months indictments were popping out of Pittsburgh like bingo balls at a church party. Before it was over, Thornburgh and his men were responsible for more than one hundred indictments against racketeers, gamblers, dope peddlers and corrupt civil servants who infested Western Pennsylvania.

The heat was on. Among those caught and later successfully prosecuted were Jeannette, Pennsylvania's Mayor Michael A. Riehl and Police Chief Arthur Rinaldi. They were guilty of fixing illegal numbers operations in their community.

Bobby Ianelli was another crook who became a casualty in Thornburgh's war. Ianelli's betting ring raked in $8 million a year from bets on professional, college and high school sports. His conviction was the first in the nation to be based on court-authorized wiretaps.

The 1970 Organized Crime Control Act was in Thornburgh's corner as it gave United States Attorneys the authority to launch major crackdowns on organized crime, using methods that were previously off-limits to federal prosecutors. Never in the history of the United States had so much muscle been flexed behind federal probes of organized crime. Thornburgh used every weapon to which he was legally entitled against the Mob. He perceived organized crime as a "business"—a lucrative business that supplied goods and services to the American public and at the same time destroyed the country.

Newark, New Jersey, in Thornburgh's opinion, was "the writing on the wall." There, the Mob brought the city to its knees before the state retaliated in the late sixties and early seventies and "cleaned up the streets."

"Organized Crime operates 365 days a year," Thornburgh often remarked in his public speeches, sometimes numbering three a week in the early years of his job as United States Attorney. "Organized crime has a board of directors with twelve or fifteen national leaders who meet whenever there's a crisis and settle feuds between some twenty-four families." Thornburgh was careful not to call the Mob, the Mafia. "That's a shorthand term," he explained to his audiences. "It's a newspaperman's word and it's not fair to Italian-Americans."

As United States Attorney Thornburgh came to know more and more about organized crime, he was appalled by the Mob's influence and meddling. Thornburgh encouraged the Pittsburgh Chamber of Commerce to issue a directory of all mob-infiltrated businesses operating in the city. A similar directory had been published and distributed in Chicago. "That way, if anyone wants to do business with these people, he'll at least know what he's up against," Thornburgh said. He believed it was essential to educate the public about organized crime and he did more teaching than any prior United States Attorney in Pittsburgh. "Unless we remove the cancer of organized crime, we will have dying communities . . . communities where moral rot sets in, because when you have officials on the take, the word spreads fast."

Despite threats against Thornburgh's life, his probe gained momentum. He looked into the affairs of the Allegheny District Attorney's office and discovered that the Anti-Racket Squad, which had existed to *neutralize* the rackets, was accepting a $500-a-month protection fee from local racketeers! Before Thornburgh finished his investigation into the District Attorney's Office, the then District Attorney Robert W. Duggan put a twelve-gauge shotgun to his head and pulled the trigger. He was found dead outside his summer home in Westmoreland County. Ninety minutes later, unaware of his death, Thornburgh's Federal Grand Jury indicted Duggan for tax evasion. He had allegedly accepted protection fees amounting to a quarter of a million dollars during more than ten years as District Attorney.

Ironically, the tips that led Thornburgh to Duggan's office had come from racketeers who were snatched in the federal crackdown on Tony Grosso's numbers combine. Grosso had been linked to John Sebastian LaRocca in the Susce Report, and his numbers racket earned more than $12 million annually in Pittsburgh and paid more than $50,000 a year in protection money to policemen and district attorneys. While the Grosso combine represented only a fraction of the $350-million numbers profit in Pennsylvania, Grosso was a major syndicate kingpin and Thornburgh sent him to prison after a lengthy and well-publicized trial.

The mobsters of Allegheny County felt the heat from Richard L. Thornburgh, whom they called "Number One Fed," but Thornburgh was less of a threat to them than a "singing" gangster. If a gangster like Grosso, for example, had chosen to bargain with the Feds, he could have dealt a serious blow to organized crime in Allegheny County with one revealing confession. So the Mob decided to protect itself.

While Nick Ferrantino was awaiting trial in Pittsburgh, where he intended to testify against several of his fellow racketeers, he was slain in a parking lot in Elyria, Ohio.

Thornburgh had moved his key witness to Elyria as a protective measure, but the Mob snuffed him out.

Not long thereafter, another Pittsburgh racketeer by the name of Alphonse Morano was gunned down in rural Allegheny County. The Mob felt he had become "too chummy" with IRS agents who were snooping into a Mob-controlled prostitution and gambling ring.

The Mob also liquidated Pittsburgh racketeer Abe Zeid. He was convicted of extortion one afternoon and shot to death the following day. The Mob feared he had an itch to "sing."

Thornburgh interpreted the gangland murders to mean, "Keep your mouth shut and live." And he worried that they would interfere with his war on crime. But even Richard L. Thornburgh underestimated himself. His probe was more effective than he had thought. As a result, the influence of what Thornburgh called the racket-politico complex in Western Pennsylvania was much weakened though it was not neutralized. "We're never going to put the rackets out of business, because they thrive on the public's desire to use illegal goods and services," Thornburgh said one evening in Pittsburgh. "We can only hope to cramp their style and keep the heat on."

No one doubted, however, that Thornburgh had come close to nabbing the crime lords of Western Pennsylvania, whose convictions could have crippled the racket-politico complex. Even John Sebastian LaRocca was in awe of Richard L. Thornburgh. One afternoon following a trial in Federal Court, the don walked up to the Number One Fed and said, "You're doin' a good job, Mr. Thornburgh. Keep it up."

Thornburgh didn't know exactly how to take "the Rock's" remark, but he thanked him, as though it had been complimentary, and smiled boyishly in the old don's direction. Thornburgh knew, of course, that LaRocca was the reputed leader of organized crime in Southwestern Pennsylvania.

That much he had learned from the Pennsylvania Crime Commission, but he had garnered even more of his knowledge about LaRocca from the tattered and aged Susce Report.

In the beginning of his tenure as United States Attorney, during those nights when Thornburgh scoured his federal files, studying prior convictions and analyzing cases, his inquisitive eyes focused on the Susce Report. It had been untouched since 1955, when Malcolm Anderson and Hubert Teitelbaum had used the document, but Thornburgh pulled it out if its dusty folder and began to read. He had remembered seeing the newspaper headlines about the Susce Report in the mid-fifties, but he knew nothing about its details or about the man who had written it. Thornburgh spent an evening paging through the report, reading Susce's odd prose and noting the names of prominent racketeers and public servants. Struggling to make sense of the document, Thornburgh scanned the newspaper clippings about Susce and the IRS following the probes of Senator John J. Williams and then Malcolm Anderson.

Eventually, Thornburgh pieced together the Susce Report and he was shocked by its overall effect. "My God," Thornburgh confided to an aide, "this was explosive. If this report had been followed up when it was written, back in the mid-forties, they could have put organized crime out of business in Pittsburgh."

Unfortunately, after twenty-five years, the clout of the Susce Report had been left behind in some file drawer in Philadelphia. Nonetheless, Thornburgh recognized its value and considered the document good background material for many of his cases against the racketeers and venal civil servants of Pittsburgh. At last, the Susce Report was being used for the purpose for which it had been originally intended: to neutralize the rackets in Pittsburgh.

Predictably, one afternoon in 1969, Andrew Susce entered the Federal Building in search of his champion. Not bothering to look in on his old IRS colleagues, Susce walked up to the United States Attorney's offices and asked to see Richard L. Thornburgh.

"I'm sure he'll want to see me," Susce urged the secretary. "I'm vitally important to him."

United States Attorney Thornburgh practiced an "open door policy" and Susce was ushered in to see him.

"Mr. Thornburgh," Susce greeted the daring prosecutor, "I'm the man who wrote the famous Susce Report and I was fired by my government for it. That was a violation of my rights. You know that. And I think that since you're using my report to put away all these gangsters, you ought to represent me before the government. Take my case to Washington, Mr. Thornburgh. I've been persecuted, my family has suffered and now I want justice. I want my good name restored and I want a pension and compensation for all my years of suffering."

Susce's plea left Thornburgh puzzled, but the United States Attorney was sympathetic to the old man. He said he wanted to help. "But Mr. Susce, this is the Justice Department. Your complaint is with the Treasury Department and there's nothing that I can do for you. I wish that I could. Your report is of historical value in assessing how the rackets developed in the western part of Pennsylvania. It's been a source of interest to us here and a reference point in carrying forth our investigations. I'm grateful for that. But I suggest that you seek legal counsel to help you in getting redress from the Treasury Department, because there's nothing that I can do."

Susce persisted while Thornburgh gave him ample time to state his case, but the United States Attorney could not help him. "I can't do a thing for you legally," Thornburgh explained, "but if it'll help you, I'll write a letter in support of your case. You've been mistreated by the government and I do think something should be done in your case, but I'm not the person to do it. I'm sorry."

Sorry, in Susce's opinion, was an inappropriate word. Why should the United States Attorney in Pittsburgh use the Susce Report when the government consistently failed to recognize its worth, or the integrity of the man who had written it? Wasn't it a contradiction for the government to use in its behalf that which it said had no substantive value? Richard L. Thornburgh, twenty-five years after the fact, continued to demonstrate that the Susce Report was accurate. "Isn't that enough proof for them to vindicate me?" Susce asked. "Can't the government admit that I was right and that they were wrong?"

Thornburgh could not disagree with his sixty-four-year-old visitor, but even so, he repeated, "There's nothing I can do."

Disappointed, Susce left Thornburgh's office, having failed again to procure a champion for his cause. But he was not defeated. Now that he knew Thornburgh was sympathetic, but ineffectual, there would have to be a new approach to his campaign. From what he read in the newspapers and watched on his television screen, Susce sensed that in the decade of the seventies the American people would unite to challenge the irresponsible and dishonest officials who cluttered the nation's bureaucracy all the way from the grassroots offices to the White House. So long as someone could be found to awaken them and provide a sense of urgency. Then, possibly then, the Government of the United States could be forced to pay attention to cases like his. He would still need a champion, of course, but he had one. He had always had one. Himself.

CHAPTER NINE

# Letters and More Letters

There were three distinguishing characteristics about Newton Falls, Ohio, in 1969. First, it was the only town in the nation with the zip code 44444. Second, it boasted one of Ohio's oldest covered bridges. Third, on one of its tiny side streets, in an oversized red brick house, lived a bitter old man named Andy Susce.

Bitter was the best adjective to describe Andy Susce. Frustrated was not entirely accurate. Angry was passé. He was bitter. The United States Government had maliciously fired him, and deprived him of his home-life and his career. Worst of all, the Government had stripped him of his pride. He was ashamed. Not for himself, for he had done nothing wrong, but for his country, which boasted the ideals of righteousness and justice. He was betrayed, he felt, and as long as the Government refused to admit its transgression, the bitterness would swell inside him. His only wish in life was to clear his name. That much he had to do. He wanted a pension and a fat compensation check, too, but the restoration of the Susce name was paramount.

Alone now, with only the support of his wife, Agnes, who had never for a moment doubted her husband, Susce planned his campaign against the Government of the United States. He remembered the advice of Attorney Sherman: "Create strong public sentiment, Andy; that will win your case because the people can force the politicians to do things that they otherwise choose to ignore." United States Attorney Thornburgh had offered similar advice. Neither of these attorneys, however, had told him exactly *how* to "create strong public sentiment," but Susce wasn't totally bewildered. The media had always impressed him as *the* vehicle for stirring up the public. He had seen it during World War II and later during the McCarthy era.

Perhaps he could convince *The New York Times* to write about him. Or *Newsweek*. Possibly he could snag the attention of Walter Cronkite on the Evening News or Mike Wallace on Sixty Minutes. Maybe a book. Or a movie. The thoughts competed for Susce's attention as he sat in his comfortably furnished front room, where in one dimly lit corner his wife had so devoutly placed a colorful statue of the Madonna with outstretched arms. The room was Susce's sanctuary. He prayed there, every morning. Some nights, the family recited the rosary there, with Andy, on bent knees, leading the Hail Marys and the Glory Bes. Praying, of course, for justice.

While he sat pondering, eager to make his campaign effectual, Susce concluded that he could not take his case to the media. *The New York Times* was four hundred miles east of Newton Falls, Ohio. And there was the problem of explaining an ordeal that had absorbed more than twenty-five years of his life, including the months he spent sleuthing for the Government. It would cost thousands of dollars to duplicate his report and his letters and his memoranda, and then mail them to reporters who might or might not help him "create strong public sentiment." Taking his case to the media, for the moment at least, was too chancy. He'd have to attract the media to his case.

Susce explored a second avenue for his vindication. He decided to launch a letter writing campaign and contact every Congressman and Senator, the President, the Vice President, legislative aides, state representatives, Governors, the Internal Revenue Service, the Civil Service Commission, the American Civil Liberties Union—anyone and any organization whose curiosity might be aroused by his case. Even a letter writing campaign would cost thousands of dollars in postage, stationery, copy machines and telephone bills, but when he finished, Susce thought, he would have informed several hundred bureaucrats—many of them servants of the people—about the Susce Report and the circumstances surrounding his unjust treatment by the Government of the United States. Someone in that group might take up the battle on his behalf.

While a letter writing campaign was probably the least effective way to "create strong public sentiment," and one that would require much time and effort, Susce was committed to it. One of his first letters in 1969 was sent to Congressman Gerald R. Ford, who was already familiar with the Susce Report, and therefore, Susce concluded, was the most likely legislator to expedite his case.

Congressman Ford replied in June, 1969:

*"Dear Andy, Thank you for your letter with all the attachments* [Susce had mailed the Congressman copies of newspaper clippings from 1955 which reported the Grand Jury investigation of his case.] *As always, it was good to hear from you . . . I appreciate your making this information available to me. I will be discussing this matter with the President the next time I talk with him at our leadership meeting. My very best wishes to you for good health and happiness."* The letter was signed, *Gerry Ford.*

Susce was elated, of course, when Ford's letter reached his

home in Newton Falls. If Congressman Ford thought enough of his case to discuss it with President Nixon, then the letter campaign, Susce reasoned, merited his dedication. He could expect, he thought, certain redress from the Government.

Another of Susce's letters was mailed to Rose Mary Woods, President Nixon's secretary, who was later suspected of erasing the President's tapes during the Watergate probe. Susce asked Miss Woods to take his case to the President and reinforce Congressman Ford's anticipated presentation. Miss Woods was not attentive.

*"Dear Mr. Susce: In Miss Woods' absence, I want you to know that your letter has reached the White House,"* read the response in August, 1969. *"Also, as you know, we have received the registered letter you sent on May 1."* Noble M. Melencamp, Staff Assistant to the President, signed the letter for Miss Woods, but he didn't say whether or not Susce's mail would be brought to the President's attention.

Also in August, Susce wrote to Congressman Robert J. Corbett of Pittsburgh, a member of the Post Office and Civil Service Committee. Susce thought that if his case were presented to that committee, he might get positive results from the Civil Service Commission. But Congressman Corbett thought otherwise:

*"My suggestion would be to ascertain what sort of appeal you can file either with the Internal Revenue Service or the Attorney General. After you have filed a formal application, if you send me a carbon copy of it I will be happy to support it with whatever efforts are most appropriate. I await your reply and wish you the best of luck."*

Of course, Susce had already tried to contact the Attorney General but his office routinely passed Susce's letters to the Treasury Department, from whence came the tired reply: *"Mr. Susce was fired for insubordination. His rights were not violated. The case is closed."* Mr. Corbett, Susce thought, was naive about the efficiency of a bureaucracy.

Even if Rose Mary Woods wasn't interested in presenting

## Letters and More Letters / 175

Susce's case to President Nixon, she didn't discourage Susce from writing directly to the President. After all, Susce had vigorously campaigned for Nixon in Trumbull County, Ohio.

But again, Noble M. Melencamp, the assistant, responded to Susce's letter. *"Thank you for your letter to President Nixon. All that you say has been noted and your correspondence is being brought to the attention of the officials of the Department of Justice. With best wishes . . ."*

Susce had expected more than the standard White House response from his friend, Dick Nixon. He knew, however, that ultimately the White House would pass his letter to the Department of Justice, and that office would pass it to the Treasury Department, from where it would be directed to the IRS Personnel Office . . . Eventually, Susce also knew, he would receive a response to the effect that "Your case is considered closed."

As the war in Viet Nam escalated, and students revolted on campuses across America, Susce grew stronger in his own campaign. The people were rising, just as he had predicted.

Again, he wrote the Honorable Gerald R. Ford. *"I have not heard from you,"* he told the Congressman, *"and you promised me that you would take my case to the President of the United States. Have you?"*

Ford responded cautiously in the spring of 1970. He said he was grateful for Susce's letter and "You may be sure that I will have your comments in mind." But he ignored the question in Susce's letter.

Another of Susce's dispatches went to Warren Olney III, the man who had headed the Justice Department's division on organized crime and had urged United States Attorney Malcolm Anderson to pursue the circumstances surrounding the Susce Report in 1955.

By 1970, Olney had been retired for several years but Susce's mail reached him at his home in Berkeley, California.

In the Summer of 1970, Olney answered: *"When I re-*

*ceived your letter, I did not at first recognize your name, but after I had read Senator Williams' remarks as printed in the Congressional Record, I did recall the Susce Report and the controversy over its disappearance from the Treasury files. I recall also that eventually we in the Justice Department obtained what we believed to be a true copy of the report and that our investigations convinced us that the report was truthful.*

Olney said the Susce Report was of major concern to him because of the issue raised over which government agency had jurisdiction to investigate it.

*"There were a number of cases, the Susce Report on John LaRocca being one, where there were allegations of criminal conduct on the part of Treasury Agents. I agreed with Senator Williams that no agency of the Federal Government should be required or allowed to investigate allegations of criminal conduct on the part of its own employees except perhaps on the most minor offenses. I thought all these allegations should be investigated by the FBI rather than by Treasury agents, but the law was far from clear on the subject and the FBI refused to accept jurisdiction . . . I am sure the FBI never did accept jurisdiction to investigate the suppression and disappearance of the Susce Report and think the reason must have been because the matter was so very old."*

Susce had requested the former Assistant Attorney General to help reinstate him in the Internal Revenue Service.

*"This I am unable to do,"* Olney continued. *"I left the Department of Justice nearly thirteen years ago and have not been in any federal service for two years. I have no personal acquaintances with any of the persons now in the Justice and Treasury Departments . . . I regret that I am unable to provide you with any help."*

Again, Susce turned his attention to the White House. He sent another registered letter to President Nixon, demanding that the Susce case be reopened and that he be reinstated.

"Thank you for your letter," came the response from Washington. "Please be assured that your opinions have been noted and that I am grateful for your observations. With best wishes, I am, Murray Chotiner, Special Counsel to the President."

On the same day that he had written to President Nixon, Susce had also mailed several other letters, including one to his friend, Gerry Ford. Susce wanted to know when Ford planned to speak with President Nixon about the Susce Report.

*"Dear Andy, It was so kind of you to write me . . . and I want to thank you for your kind personal comments and for your interest in the Republican cause. May I also thank you for sending me the clipping from the Newton Falls Herald relative to your appearance on the Pittsburgh television station. I trust that your appearance and the accompanying publicity will be helpful to your cause. Warmest personal regards. Gerry."*

Oddly enough, in 1970, KDKA television contacted Susce and invited him to appear on a program devoted to organized crime in Pittsburgh. KDKA's Larry Schmidt, who was the commentator, introduced Susce to the Pittsburgh television audience as "the man who twenty-seven years ago challenged the Mafia head on as a Zone Deputy Collector for the Internal Revenue Service." Schmidt said that Susce had investigated John Sebastian LaRocca, who was consistently mentioned throughout the documentary as the crime boss of Southwestern Pennsylvania.

During Susce's interview, he related the circumstances of the LaRocca investigation and the writing of the Susce Report. He mentioned the confession of Joseph Brusco; the ledgers of Angotti; and the meeting with LaRocca when the don admitted that he had bilked the Government and offered to pay whatever taxes he owed. Susce also related that IRS Collector Stanley Granger ordered him to "rewrite the report or burn it" and, following his refusal to do so, he was fired before a kangaroo court in August, 1944.

"Susce learned," Schmidt said at the conclusion of his interview, "that the power of the Mafia is not to be taken lightly . . . the United States Government has to exert all its influences to accomplish anything against the Mafia . . . Mafiosi are presented as harmless, romantic figures deserving of sympathy and respect. But it's a myth that the Mafia is a bunch of nice guys being picked on by the police."

Other guests on Schmidt's documentary, which ran as a series for several evenings in Pittsburgh, included Richard L. Thornburgh, United States Attorney. Thornburgh explained that racketeers paid lawmakers more money each month to keep them crooked than honest citizens—taxpayers—paid to keep them honest. He mentioned the Susce Report and told the Pittsburgh audience that while Susce's allegations were specific, no action was taken following the report because "the racketeers had access to the Internal Revenue Service and the structure of the system, including the police and other federal and state agents."

This publicity, as Congressman Ford had written, should have aided Susce's cause, but there were no immediate results. Television viewers who followed the series were outraged by Schmidt's revelations and they sympathized with Susce, who suffered while LaRocca and his gang continued their freewheeling, corrupt lifestyles, but no one did anything about it.

The KDKA series was not entirely a loss for Susce's campaign, however. Shortly after his appearance on the program he was contacted by a second member of the fourth estate who wanted to write an article about him for the *Cleveland Plain Dealer*, Ohio's leading morning newspaper.

Mairy Jayne Woge was the *Plain Dealer*'s crime reporter in Eastern Ohio and Western Pennsylvania. When she met

Susce at his home to interview him, she told him she had heard of his case on the KDKA documentary, and that she had read the Susce Report in Thornburgh's office. She wanted to assist Susce's battle against the Government.

At last, to Susce's delight, the press had come to him. The timing was perfect. His own letter writing campaign would mesh with the publicity of the fourth estate, he said, and "create strong public sentiment."

Woge's article ran across page one of the *Plain Dealer*. She summarized Susce's story, playing up the injustice, and then explained how the whistleblower was seeking vindication. The article was a good dramatic narrative, but it resulted in silence. Woge told Susce that she would send the piece to Attorney General John Mitchell, whom she knew personally, and to various members of Congress, whom she hoped to convince to intervene for Andy Susce. Apparently her efforts weren't any better rewarded than Schmidt's, or Susce's, for Susce did not hear from her again.

Susce continued his letter campaign through 1970, and then decided to take advantage of his political contacts. Susce had served as Vice-Chairman of the election committee for United States Senator Robert Taft, Jr., in Trumbull County, Ohio. The Chairman of the committee was William B. Maurice, and he agreed to write to Senator Taft and persuade him to assist Susce.

"*Dear Senator Taft: I have reviewed the attached material regarding Andrew Susce's report and believe his case merits your personal attention.*

"*Your file on this matter may be more complete than mine* [Susce had previously written to Taft] *but on the basis of what I have seen and heard he deserves vindication.*

"*I'm not sure if you are aware of Mr. Susce's work on your behalf as Vice-chairman of the Trumbull Country Taft-for-Senate Committee in the 1970 election. In the face of strong local party opposition in the primary, you will recall that we turned a sure Rhodes County into a 3500 majority Taft County.*

*"In my personal opinion, there is political value to Mr. Susce's crusade against unwanted elements in our system.*

*"But the humanitarian aspects of this victim of the 'bureaucracy' deserves your personal consideration."*

Maurice's letter moved Senator Taft to contact the Treasury Department about Susce's file.

Predictably, the Director of the Personnel Division of the Treasury Department responded negatively:

*" Dear Senator Taft: Mr. Susce was discharged from the position of Zone Deputy Collector, Pittsburgh, Pennsylvania, on October 16, 1944. The charge against Mr. Susce was that he had made unfounded accusations against a superior officer and the four specifications under the charge detailed his allegations that the 'U.S. Collector' was violating the Internal Revenue Laws of the United States.*

*"This charge was an outgrowth of Mr. Susce's refusal to complete his assigned duties and his persistence in making unauthorized and exploratory investigations as a Deputy Collector. A complete investigation exonerated the official against whom Mr. Susce had leveled charges reflecting upon the official's integrity. The removal action was approved by the Office of the Secretary of the Treasury and further appeal was taken to the Civil Service Commission with the Commission sustaining the removal.*

*"Over the past twenty-seven years, Mr. Susce had contacted various members of the Senate and the House of Representatives with a view towards obtaining reinstatement. This correspondence has precipitated several reviews of the case, all resulting in sustention of his removal.*

*"We have, several times in the past, informed Mr. Susce that the Internal Revenue Service and the Office of the Secretary consider his case a closed issue. Having once again re-*

*viewed Mr. Susce's file, we have concluded that there is no basis or justification for reversing the original decision to remove him from the Service. I regret that the facts in the case preclude a more favorable reply."*

Senator Taft immediately notified Susce of the Treasury Department's letter and wrote that he was sorry, but the case was closed.

Tears rolled down Susce's face when he read this latest letter from the Treasury Department. It was the most detailed account ever released in explanation of his dismissal, and it left him trembling. "How can they say that I made 'unfounded accusations against a superior officer' and that I conducted 'unauthorized and exploratory investigations as a Deputy Collector'? They're lying. They're *lying*," he shouted in his desperation as he paced the floor in his front room.

Obviously, the government had ignored the facts of Susce's accusations, as well as those of his dismissal, and had instead pointed the finger at the whistleblower. The Treasury people disregarded the fact that Susce's report had been ditched in a file drawer for ten years where it would have remained permanently buried had it not been for Senator John J. Williams' insistence that it be found.

And furthermore, if the report had been unauthorized, then why did Stanley Granger tell the Grand Jury that he had forwarded the Susce Report to the Intelligence Division for investigation? Why, in 1955, hadn't he said the Susce Report was "unauthorized" if, indeed, that were true?

"Don't they realize that I was set up?" Susce cried. "Can't they see that Granger lied about me so that I could be fired and blackballed? Isn't there any justice left in this country?"

Gradually, Susce's despair turned to strength and he faced the full reality of his discouraging situation. He wrote a letter to Senator Taft.

*"Dear Senator: I received your letter dated November 2, 1971. This type of letter from you has been received two years*

*ago which indicates your file is not consistant* [sic] *and up to date or you have misleading information. Here are the real reasons why my case would* [sic] *be brought to the floor of the U.S. Senate by you."*

Susce then outlined a dozen points which he considered central to his case. He reiterated the revelations of Senator Williams' probe; the 1955 Grand Jury investigation which had sought to issue presentments but was prevented from doing so by Malcolm Anderson; the letter from Olney which explained that the Susce Report was accurate; and KDKA's documentary which included Thornburgh's statement that Susce had been unjustly fired because the Mob had infiltrated the IRS and other federal offices.

*"So Senator you have some of the pertainet* [sic] *facts which you can introduce for me on the Senate floor. I and my associates here in Trumbull County put you in as U.S. Senator from Ohio to* [sic] *but if you didn't make it in the primary you would be cut."*

In concluding his letter, Susce informed Taft that it was his obligation to introduce a private bill for the relief of his constituent, Andrew Susce. "I deserve to be reinstated and compensated for my suffering these past twenty-seven years."

While awaiting Senator Taft's reply, Susce mailed a letter to J. Edgar Hoover of the FBI, and he also sent two additional letters, several days apart, to Congressman Ford.

Hoover responded immediately. "Since the facts stated in your recent communication do not pertain to any matter within the investigative jurisdiction of the FBI, I have referred it to the Commissioner, Internal Revenue Service . . . Very truly yours," signed, J. Edgar Hoover.

Congressman Ford responded: "Dear Andy, I want to thank you for sending me the copy of the article from The Plain Dealer . . . The article was well written and I do hope it will have the proper effect. My very best wishes to you."

Ford's response to Susce's second letter arrived several days later: "Thank you for your letter and enclosure regarding the indictment of Meyer Lansky and his connection with Mr. Albert Parvin. I appreciate your support and am confident that the full truth in this curious case will eventually come out. Kind personal regards, Gerry."

"Why won't Ford help me?" Susce asked his wife after reading Ford's second letter. "I've been writing to him for twenty years and he keeps telling me that he'll help me but he never does nothing. Yes, mine is a 'curious case,' but it's even more curious why he doesn't do something about it."

Finally, in December, 1971, Susce received the anxiously awaited response from Senator Taft. It was one paragraph. "Dear Mr. Susce: I have carfully reviewed your file and do not believe a private bill would be of any assistance to you. With kind regards," Robert Taft, Jr.

Early in 1972, Susce renewed his plea to Senator Taft. "Why won't you introduce a bill for me?" he persisted.

The Senator's response was a classic:

*"Dear Mr. Susce: I have once again reviewed your entire file and can appreciate the heartbreak, frustration and anguish which you have experienced relative to this matter. It is surely little comfort to you to know that many Americans commend you for the courageous stand which you have taken, when it jeopardized your own employment.*

*"Just as you have been honest and forthright, I must also be candid with you. The Judiciary Committee to which private bills such as yours are referred is not responsive to this type of private bill. If I were to introduce a bill it would only give you a false encouragement which is not what you need at this time. Had this matter occurred two or three years ago, the likelihood of legislative remedies would be greatly enhanced. But now, after approximately twenty years [sic], I cannot encourage you in thinking that there will be legislative relief.*

*Obviously, this is not the answer which you seek and it is not an answer which I would be content with were I in your position, but I believe that I should be completely honest with you. I am sorry that I was not in the Senate years ago so that I could have taken this matter up when it was more timely.*

"*You have, if nothing more, the personal satisfaction of knowing that you did what you knew to be right and this is one of the greatest satisfactions that any man can have.*" Signed, *Robert Taft, Jr.*

Senator Taft had taken Susce's plea for vindication and turned it into his own plea for Susce to take his problems elsewhere. Perhaps the Senator thought his compassion could wrestle Susce loose of his obsession, but of course he was wrong. In Susce's estimation, the letter was ludicrous. The line "had this matter occurred two or three years ago, the likelihood of legislative remedies would be greatly enhanced" was particularly annoying to him. What difference did it make when the injustice occurred—shouldn't it still be rectified? The line "I am only sorry that I was not in the Senate years ago so that I could have taken this matter up when it was more timely" was rhetoric to someone like Susce. Timeliness had never been a prerequisite of justice.

Nevertheless, Taft's letter was at least favorable to Susce's cause. It was a verification that Susce had acted "courageously" and "jeopardized" his job. He made copies of Taft's commendation and sent them to the dozens of names that now appeared on his mailing list.

Mail flowed with regularity between Susce's home in Newton Falls and Washington, D.C., but Congressional leaders and President Nixon weren't the only names on his mailing list. Consistently, Susce also wrote to the Internal Revenue Service and the Civil Service Commission.

The latter agency always sent the same reply: "Under the circumstances, there is nothing we can do now to assist you in your cause." Occasionally, the Commission would also explain, "Under the then controlling laws and regulations governing employee appeals, you had no right to a hearing before the Civil Service Commission and the Commission had no authority to review the merits of a removal action . . ."

The IRS was even more restrained in its explanations to Susce. "As we have consistently informed you through the years, your case has been thoroughly reviewed. The reviews have consistently concluded that your removal was procedurally and meritoriously correct. Therefore, your case is considered closed."

Susce refused to believe that he "had no right to a hearing before the Civil Service Commission" but otherwise, he agreed, his removal was *procedurally* correct. "But that's not the issue, damn it. I'm a victim in this mess. They followed all the rules, but they didn't listen to what I was saying. They just wanted to get rid of me, and they did."

By 1974, the year that Watergate busted Richard M. Nixon and the Republicans, and pushed Gerald R. Ford into the White House, Susce was forced to admit to himself that his letter campaign had failed.

Remembering that William B. Maurice had been instrumental in persuading Senator Taft to pursue his case with the Treasury people, Susce contacted another GOP friend in Trumbull County and asked if he'd contribute his influence to the letter campaign.

Attorney E. G. Ted Johnson was the chairman of Trumbull County's Republican Executive Committee, and Susce had met him at campaign headquarters during the Nixon years. Johnson was admired by his friends in Eastern Ohio and he was influential in Republican circles, including those that revolved around state and national figures. Susce asked if he would write a letter for him to William B. Saxbe, an Ohioan who had suddenly been appointed Attorney General. "Now's my chance," Susce told Johnson, excitedly. "A Republican Attorney General who's also an Ohioan will jump on this case."

Johnson eagerly obliged his friend Susce:

"*Dear Bill,*" the attorney wrote Saxbe in the summer of 1974, "*I have a Republican Precinct Committeeman here in Newton Falls, Trumbull County by the name of Andrew J. Susce who has a very important personal matter involving the United States Department of Treasury and the Internal Revenue Service. He has attempted to get the matter straightened out which problem* [sic] *goes back some twenty years and I have suggested that he have a personal interview with you relative to the matter. I suggested that he call your office to make an appointment to see you, which he did last week. However, he has asked me to submit a letter to you following up his request.*

"*I would appreciate it very much if you would see this gentleman and see if something can be done for him. He is a very hard worker for the Republican Party in this County and has been a supporter of Republican candidates for many many years.*" The letter was signed, *Ted*.

Perhaps it was the "very hard worker for the Republican Party" phrase that prompted Saxbe to assign one of his counselors to follow up on the letter from the Ohio attorney. William M. Hoiles replied from Washington and asked Johnson to instruct Susce to "give me a call, I will be more than happy to meet with him." Hoiles also asked for additional information about the Susce case.

In September, 1974, Johnson sent Hoiles a detailed chronology of the Susce case.

"*I believe that Mr. Susce was given a most unreasonable form of treatment by the Government, and he has been trying for almost thirty years to rectify the situation, but has had a complete run-around in this matter,*" Johnson said in the letter that accompanied the chronology to Washington.

*"I have gone over the documents enclosed, and refer you particularly to the copy of the Cleveland Plain Dealer article. I feel that Mr. Susce should have his record cleared, that he should be compensated for back pay, damages, and pension adjustment, as well as being awarded a jeopardy assessment on the tax matter [against LaRocca].*

*"I trust that you will make arrangements with him for a personal interview, and if required, I will also appear as his legal counsel . . . My best to the Attorney General."* Signed, Ted Johnson.

About two months later, Hoiles requested additional information about Susce and his "curious case."

"I knew Mr. Saxbe would jump on this," Susce said confidently to Johnson.

The attorney wrote a third letter to Hoiles, providing the additional materials. "I am requesting you as a personal friend to see if something cannot be done for this man in the form of some sort of recognition and compensation," Johnson urged Hoiles.

Several months later, Attorney Johnson's influence in the Justice Department was crimped when William Saxbe was sent to India as an Ambassador. He vacated his office almost as suddenly as he had assumed it, serving less than a year. At any rate, Hoiles was never heard from again.

By this time, however, Susce's case had hooked Johnson and he continued to assist in Susce's campaign. In 1975, Johnson wrote a letter to Richard L. Thornburgh, who that year was promoted to Assistant Attorney General and Chief of the Justice Department's war on organized crime. It was the same position that earlier had been held by Warren Olney III, and after him, Malcolm Anderson.

Johnson opened his letter by saying, *"I imagine that you are already aware of the problem that I am going to outline in this letter, but this thing has developed into a situation that has considerable political overtones . . ."* For several paragraphs Johnson briefed Thornburgh about the recent developments in Susce's battle with the Government. He emphasized that Susce continued to fight for vindication. "*[Andrew Susce is] a person who has helped all our Republican candidates during the past several elections,*" Johnson informed Thornburgh. "*I will sincerely appreciate any help that you can give to Mr. Susce by having some arrangements made to compensate him for his suffering.*"

Thornburgh responded in one paragraph. As he had explained to Susce several years past, the Susce case was a matter for the Treasury Department and not the Department of Justice. He apologized that he could not be of assistance.

While Johnson attempted, unsuccessfully, to rouse patronage support, Susce continued writing letters from his home in Newton Falls. Now that his friend, Gerry Ford, was in the White House, Susce assumed that the President would remember his "curious case" and rectify the blistering injustice that the government had been hiding behind for more than thirty years. "Now that Gerry's in the White House," Susce told Agnes, "he has the authority to do something for me. Look what he did for Nixon."

In the spring of 1975, Susce sent President Ford a letter and asked if he had made any progress with the Susce case.

Jay T. French, assistant counsel for the President, replied enlighteningly in March, 1975:

"*Dear Mr. Susce: Thank you for your letter . . . By checking into the facts of your case, I learned that former Senator Williams of Delaware called attention to the circumstances surrounding your discharge from employment at the Internal Revenue Service in a message to the United States Senate on June 23, 1953. A copy of the Congressional Record containing his remarks is enclosed for your record. Also, the United States Attorney in Pittsburgh has confirmed that the work you did in the 1940s proved subsequently to be very important to the Federal Government. With appreciation. Sincerely, Jay T. French."*

Susce was amused that French should send him a copy of Senator Williams' remarks in the *Congressional Record,* as if the old man had not known the record existed. He was certain that had French looked into President Ford's congressional files, he would have found that years before it was Andy Susce who had sent a copy of the Senator's remarks to Congressman Ford. No matter, however. The letter from Jay T. French was the closest that Susce had come to vindication. At last the White House admitted the Susce Report "proved subsequently to be very important to the Federal Government." Now, he thought, how could the Government continue to deny his vindication when counsel for the President of the United States had acknowledged the value of the Susce Report? After reading French's letter, Susce believed for the first moment in many years, that his battle was about to be won.

A few days following the arrival of French's letter, Attorney Johnson responded to the White House and requested "adequate compensation for Mr. Susce for the injustices done to him."

French did not acknowledge the letter. After several weeks, Johnson wrote a second letter. When by July, 1975, he had still not heard from French, the attorney wrote a third time. None of the letters was ever acknowledged and suddenly Susce realized that he was back to zero.

Susce drafted a letter to Senator Howard H. Baker, Jr., asking that Baker's committee, the Senate Select Committee on Intelligence Activities, consider the Susce case. Senator Baker replied, "I can assure you that your communication will be considered by the Committee in the coming weeks." If his communication *was* considered, Susce never heard about it.

Next, Susce wrote Ohio State Senator Donald E. Lukens, a personal friend, and asked him to convince the Ohio legislature to pressure the Federal Government about the Susce matter. But Lukens' response was patronizing at best. "I wish I were your Congressman, I would certainly take this case all the way. Keep peace, you have many friends and much support and I know that President Ford does appreciate the sacrifices you have made for your country."

Susce photostated the letters from Lukens and French and mailed copies to the Internal Revenue Service. Based on the letters, he petitioned the Service to reopen his case and reinstate him with compensation. Billy J. Brown, Director of the IRS Personnel Division, replied that he could not allow the claim. "It is my conclusion," he said, "that the information contained in these letters does not alter" the position of the IRS.

In 1976, Susce sent a packet of information about his case to the American Civil Liberties Union in Columbus, Ohio. That office forwarded the information to its national chapter in Washington D.C., with a cover letter that read, in part, "The General Counsel for the ACLU of Ohio, Nelson Karl, feels that the ACLU's role [in regards to the Susce case] should be limited to the single issue of his [Susce's] right to a hearing which has never been offered to him. Since this must happen in Washington, we have sent the file to you . . . Please give this matter your consideration and inform us of your intended actions."

The Washington office responded in December of 1976 and told Susce that his case would "be reviewed by a volunteer attorney and presented to our Lawyers Screening Committee . . . If the Committee decides that your case is one that we may be in a position to handle, we may then arrange for a volunteer attorney to investigate further, meet with you, and make a final determination." The letter asked that Susce

"Please be patient" as "it will require several weeks before we can be in further touch with you."

Susce waited one year, until December, 1977, and then wrote the ACLU in Washington and asked if any decision had been made about his case. John H.F. Shattuck, ACLU Director, replied, "I'm afraid I know nothing about your case or your files."

The Bicentennial year restored the spiritual strength that had been sucked from Susce in his exhausting battle. "This is the year," Susce said to Johnson. "The Government can show the country that justice lives in America, even after two hundred years. All they have to do is clear my name."

In February, 1976, Susce wrote a letter to the Internal Revenue Service and requested that his case be reopened during the Bicentiennial year and that he be awarded "pension, back-pay and damages."

Bicentennial or not, the IRS was steadfast. "We have thoroughly examined the files of the Internal Revenue Service concerning this matter and we have determined that your claim has already been adjudicated," wrote William F. Long, Jr., Chief of the Legal Services Division.

The response, of course, didn't surprise Susce—it couldn't surprise him. The IRS had long ago proved immune to all appeals.

Through the winter of 1976, and into the early spring, Susce's days were spent in his cozy front room from where he carried on his battle with the Government. He wanted to make 1976 his year. Tragically, though, this was not to be. On March 27, 1976, Agnes Susce dropped dead. She had been struck down by a heart attack.

In the mind of her widower, only one word described the cause of Agnes' death. Stress. Agnes Susce had been a healthy woman. Rarely had she suffered even a cold. There were no warnings before she died; she just collapsed. She was sixty-six years old. Susce believed that she had succumbed to the pressure of more than thirty years of his fighting the United States Government, and the thought deepened his resentment and his grief.

Agnes Susce had been deprived, really, of her husband's company. For twenty-five years he came home only on weekends. He was, sometimes, a visitor in her life; a visitor who carried a burden that stretched from Pittsburgh to Washington to Newton Falls. But Agnes had loved him. So much, in fact, that she had married him without a penny in his pocket and at the height of the nation's worst depression. She had protected him, and encouraged him. She, more than anyone, had been his source of strength.

Several days after Agnes' death, Ohio's One Hundred and Eleventh General Assembly issued a citation in her memory. The citation was sponsored by State Senator Lukens, who said, in offering the assembly's condolences to the Susce family, that Agnes was "one of Ohio's finest citizens."

A letter from President Ford also followed Agnes' death.

*"Dear Andy: Phil Buchen has passed along to me the sad news of Agnes' passing. I was very, very sorry to learn about it and hope and trust that you are becoming reconciled to so great a loss.*

*"Betty joins me in sending deepest sympathy. May God sustain you in this time of grief and sadness. Our thoughts and prayers are with you."*

Ford's letter was of little comfort to Susce, but he felt honored to have received it. He had the letter inscribed on the back of Agnes' tombstone.

Weeks passed before Susce resumed his campaign. He felt guilty when he thought of returning to the battle. It had killed his wife, he felt, and eventually it would kill him, also. For days he doubted that he could continue without Agnes. Her loss left him desolated and he wanted to die. Slowly though, he regained his wish to live, consoled by his children, and particularly by his daughter Gwendolyn, who lived at home. She led him back to the battle that had been the absorbing interest in his life for so long.

In the late spring of 1976, still counting on his vindication in the Bicentennial year, Susce asked Attorney Johnson to write a letter for him to the United States Congressman, Charles J. Carney, who represented Ohio's nineteenth district, including Newton Falls.

As he had done several times before in letters to other politicians, Johnson outlined Susce's case for the Honorable Mr. Carney. The Congressman then queried the Treasury Department about Susce's case and in June, 1976, he received a reply. It was not unlike the reply that had earlier been sent to Senator Taft.

Congressman Carney forwarded the Treasury's response to Johnson and explained that Susce's case was considered closed. He apologized for what he was sure was unhappy news.

Johnson responded in a two-page letter, attempting to refute the explanation handed down by the IRS.

*"Mr. Susce, and I might add myself, still feel that he was wrongfully dismissed from the Service, irregardless of the report that you received from the IRS . . . Mr. Susce at no time had an opportunity to present his side of the matter to any department and consequently in view of his position, the least we could ask for is a hearing of some sort before some authorized governmental body relative to his entire case.*

*"I might add that Mr. Susce's life for the past thirty some odd years has been one of total frustration over this entire matter, not only of the suppression of his report but of the fact that he was unceremoniously fired from his job without adequate hearing or anything of that sort . . . this particular matter has been a thorn in his side for these many years and it*

*appears that at least he should have the opportunity to submit his side of the entire case. I am sure that after having heard all of the facts, and a review of all the documents . . . some adequate compensation should be forthcoming."*

Congressman Carney responded with another apology. The case was closed and he could do nothing about it.

America's Bicentennial lapsed without even a hint of Susce's vindication, but he continued badgering the Government. In June of 1977, Attorney Johnson wrote a letter of appeal to President Jimmy Carter. Of course, the Democrats were back in the White House and Susce said his appeal would certainly be turned away. And it was. The President, or more accurately, one of the President's aides, forwarded Susce's appeal to the Internal Revenue Service from where it elicited a worn out response: "The case is closed."

A month after he had written to President Carter, Attorney Johnson addressed a similar plea to another Democrat, Senator Howard Metzenbaum of Ohio. The Senator promptly responded through an aide and requested that he be better appraised of the matter. Johnson sent the Ohio legislator a chronology of the Susce case, along with a copy of *Pittsburgh* magazine which several months before had featured an article about Susce and his report. In July, a follow-up article was carried in *The Nation*, and that, too, was mailed to Senator Metzenbaum.

Not long thereafter, Ellen Shifrin, the Senator's aide who had been assigned to the Susce matter, telephoned Susce and Johnson. Senator Metzenbaum was more than casually interested in the miscarriage of justice that had been leveled at Andrew Susce. Shifrin said the Senator would pursue the case to the appropriate Government agencies.

There wasn't any reason for Susce to believe Howard Metzenbaum could be any more effective than the multitude of politicians that had previously tried to crack his case at the

IRS. But he chose to hope, nonetheless. Granted, Senator Metzenbaum was a Democrat, and Susce would not have campaigned for him in Trumbull County, but in retrospect, politics had not mediated his case. Little good it had done him to campaign for Richard Nixon and Robert Taft, Jr., and Charles J. Carney and Gerald R. Ford.

Politics was not the issue here. It was justice—an ideal that was purportedly apolitical. Susce would trust in Howard Metzenbaum. And if the Senator failed him, he wouldn't abandon his campaign. No, he couldn't now. He was seventy years old; he lacked the energy of his youth, but he was healthy and he had drive. And he had time. If Senator Metzenbaum failed him, he'd continue writing letters, and more letters.

CHAPTER TEN

# The Buck Stops Where?

Since Watergate, in the early seventies, Americans have been cautious about the men and women they've elected to run the country. Like the Populists at the turn of the century, Americans by the mid-seventies demanded a grassroots, people-oriented government in which the needs of the American people would be regarded as more important than the political whims and ambitions of their representatives.

Men like Wayne Hays of Ohio discovered just how government-conscious the people had become when he was bumped into early retirement after his mistress announced that she was on his House payroll. The Hays scandal, so soon after Watergate, reinforced the country's suspicions that its leaders were immoral. Politicians everywhere were scrutinized by angry Americans who, for the first time in years, poked their noses into the "affairs" of their representatives.

Then, in 1976, along came Jimmy Carter of Georgia. His pearly-white smile, not unlike the smile of Teddy Roosevelt, and his "good ole boy" jargon, not unlike the homey jargon of

Harry Truman, appealed to the people. Among other qualities, the people responded to Jimmy's apparently simple down-to-earth nature, and they elected him their President.

On the day he was inaugurated, Jimmy Carter and his family stopped their limousine on Pennsylvania Avenue and walked several chilly blocks to the White House. It was a moving gesture, signifying that the new President stood among the people and not above them. The people could rest easier now, for President Carter was an honest man who would do only what was best for the country. There would be no John Deans or John Mitchells in the Carter Administration. There would be no one to take the blame but the President himself. As he told his fellow Americans, "The buck stops here."

Gerald R. Ford's loss to Jimmy Carter was a disappointment to Andrew Susce. Of all the politicians he had corresponded with in the previous thirty-two years, Susce thought his friend Gerry Ford would be the man to clear his name. Gerry Ford knew more about the Susce case than any politician in Washington. He had corresponded with Susce more than a dozen times in reference to his "curious case." And he had occupied the White House when Jay T. French wrote Susce and acknowledged that the Susce Report "proved subsequently to be very important to the Federal Government."

But now Gerald R. Ford was out and while there was talk that his political star would rise again, Susce couldn't count on it and he wouldn't wait. This man Carter, even though he was a Democrat, was quite unlike the sophisticated John F. Kennedy who had chosen to ignore Susce's plea for vindication. Now that Senator Howard Metzenbaum was investigating Susce's unjust firing by the Internal Revenue Service, there was, perhaps, a greater chance the new President would hear Susce's case and clear his name.

Susce's attorney, Ted Johnson, wrote a detailed letter to

President Carter, requesting him to consider Susce's case. Within several weeks, the President responded, indirectly, thereby clarifying his politics in the mind of Andrew Susce.

One of Carter's aides had simply sent Susce's letter to the Treasury Department, just as had Ford, Nixon, Johnson and Kennedy.

"It's all show," Susce told his longtime lawyer friend, Harry Alan Sherman, in Pittsburgh. "The President is not a man for the people. He's protecting the Democrats. After thirty-two years the Susce Report is still too hot to handle."

Attorney Harry Alan Sherman agreed. He sat in his tilt-back leather chair behind an almost tear-shaped walnut desk that had been cleared on top except for a brown note pad, a ballpoint pen, and a lamp dressed in symbols of freedom and justice—a liberty bell, an eagle, a flag. Portraits of his children, painted by the attorney himself, decorated the wall next to his desk. Across the room was a wall of bookshelves full of law journals as well as contemporary novels and exposés. Behind him, on top of a cabinet, was Sherman's unpublished book of poetry. He had memorized it. Occasionally he'd recite a line or a stanza to emphasize a point. Or when his poetry wouldn't do, he'd rely on his wit. "The price of liberty is eternal justice," was one of his favorite quotes.

Sherman shook his head distastefully, clutching his vest, like a farmer grasping his suspenders. "Let me tell you something," he said to Susce. "Carter is a Rockefeller Republican. Rockefeller money put him in office because the Republicans knew they couldn't win the White House in 1976. So they bought it. They called in Carter and asked him, 'Do you know who's going to be the Democratic nominee for President?' And Carter said, 'No, I don't.' 'Well it's going to be you, Jimmy Carter, and we're going to pay your way.'" Sherman told the story as though he had been in the opposite room the day Rockefeller supposedly met with the Georgian politician.

"Carter's not interested in your case. Neither is Senator Metzenbaum. I talked with his aide about the Susce Report. She called and asked me if I'd give her some details, and I did. I told her the whole story and said the time was long overdue for your name to be cleared. But Metzenbaum is only giving you lip service. And just like John Williams, the Mr. Clean in a House of Thieves, if the IRS goes after Metzenbaum he'll drop the Susce matter, too.

"A politician is the lowest form of human life—they lose their good qualities completely. Unfortunately we need them to run for office in a representative form of government. It's too bad they have to play politics, but that's what they're doing with the Susce Report. Watergate was spit on the sidewalk—that was a violation of a local ordinance—it's nothing compared with robbing hundreds and hundreds of millions of dollars from the country. To this day, our country is being robbed of that tax money by the Mafia. But it's going to take someone with character to bring the Susce matter into the open. And men with character don't stay in politics for long. Like Malcolm Anderson, when they find out they'll have to sell their souls to stay in office, they get out fast."

In downtown Pittsburgh, Malcolm Anderson was in his grand office on the seventeenth floor of the Oliver Building. Except for his hair, which had turned white, Anderson looked as fit as he had in the 1950s when he was the United States Attorney in Western Pennsylvania and later an Assistant Attorney General of the United States. Now he was the senior partner in a corporate law firm, having quit the Attorney General's office in 1959, after less than fourteen months in office.

Dressed conservatively but fashionably in a white shirt and wide, printed tie, Anderson set his feet upon the sheet of glass that covered his oversized walnut desk. He lit a cigar, peered out the tall, curtainless window to the right of him and stared at a church steeple that poked above Pittsburgh's skyline. He tried to recall the details of the Susce case.

"I can't help thinking that the Internal Revenue Service put Susce in over his head. They turned him loose on this investigation of LaRocca and then because he turned out to be more tenacious than they wanted him to be, they fired him. It was a raw deal." Anderson paused to re-light his cigar.

Like Sherman, Anderson had also been contacted by Senator Metzenbaum's office. "There seems to be some question about who told him to do the report. The Internal Revenue Service claims that it was not authorized," Anderson continued. He smiled as he reflected on the Susce Report. "When I first got the Susce thing, I thought, 'Did this fellow, on his own initiative, do this?' But later we found out that a letter had come down from J. Edgar Hoover and was eventually sent to the Treasury and then down to Pittsburgh. So I told the Senator's office that that was how it started. I don't have all the threads of it but I have always been satisfied that Susce was ordered to do the investigation. That was never challenged during the time when I was involved with the case [in 1953]."

It was typical for a man of Malcolm Anderson's convictions to stop in the midst of a complicated day and reconsider the Susce case, which was now nearly thirty-five years old. The injustice disturbed him. "If I had the authority," he said, slouching in his chair and tucking his hands inside the top of his trousers, "I would order that the Susce case be given a hearing *de novo*. It means, 'from the beginning.' Everything should be aired—what did he do wrong? What truth was there in the allegation that he did things wrong? I'm satisfied that he must have been insubordinate. It just strikes me that he was. But I think he had extenuating circumstances, and I don't think he was given a fair shake on that.

"I think we ought to reopen this case and make some determination of whether he should have been discharged. I personally think that it's a pretty dirty deal to pick a little Collector who has no expertise, and give him one of the toughest assignments that could be given to a skilled task force and then, when he turns in his report, tell him it is no more of his business, and fire him. That part of it, whether it is technically right or not, doesn't sit well with me. He deserves better treatment."

As an afterthought, Anderson said that Susce would have had a much better case "if at the end of the damn thing, we had gotten three or four big racketeers and four or five crooked IRS men. But we didn't, and that takes the punch out of it."

Anderson's memory wasn't totally accurate. John J. Williams' investigation in the early fifties had sent more than "four or five crooked IRS men" to prison. Anderson himself had sent four of Pittsburgh's IRS employees to prison in the mid-fifties. None of the swindlers had been named in the Susce Report, but their crimes, certainly, were an indication that all was not in order in the local IRS office.

Furthermore, while the racketeers in Susce's report had escaped prosecution in the forties and fifties, Richard L. Thornburgh as United States Attorney in Western Pennsylvania had put away a crop of racketeers in the late sixties and early seventies. And Thornburgh admitted that he had used the Susce Report for background information.

In 1978, Richard L. Thornburgh's office was one floor below Malcolm Anderson's in the Oliver Building. Recently back from his Washington stint as Assistant Attorney General, Thornburgh had joined a Pittsburgh law firm, but his immediate interests were in seeking the Governor's seat in Pennsylvania. One morning, dressed casually in a bulky sweater, Thornburgh sat in his modern office overlooking Mellon Square. He hadn't shaved that morning but it was Saturday and the offices were closed. Dick Thornburgh, as he preferred to be called, was working on his own time, laying strategy for his campaign. The top of his cluttered, wooden desk included legal documents, folders, scribbled notes, a stained coffee cup, a tiny, green plant and a campaign button that read, in bold print, "Happiness is a Republican Governor."

It *was* rather passé, but that didn't matter. Dick Thornburgh was otherwise original, and his reputation as an honest, dedicated civil servant set him above most political aspirants in Pennsylvania. In the May primary, he'd face six other gubernatorial hopefuls, including Philadelphia's David Marston, the fired United States Attorney who capitalized on the publicity that followed his dismissal by President Carter. Dick Thornburgh was a favorite. The people liked him and they trusted him. Pennsylvania's Mob feared him, of course, and they would not want this former "Number One Fed" in the Governor's mansion. They would try to stop him, but then they had tried before. Dick Thornburgh had never scared easily.

In his office, he paused to remember Andrew Susce. It had been several years before that Susce had visited the then United States Attorney in the Federal Building. Susce had asked the young attorney to clear his name, but Thornburgh had said he couldn't, and in 1978 he hadn't changed his mind.

"It's a matter for the Treasury Department. I often thought of what I might do, but it was a bureaucracy problem. I couldn't get the Treasury people to recognize this was a guy whose motives and instincts were proper even if he may have transcended some of the normal rules of operation. Whether he's entitled to back pay or pension is up to the Treasury people, but he wasn't treated fairly . . ."

The ramifications of Susce's case troubled Thornburgh. "I'm quite familiar with this whistleblowing thing," he said.

"A lot of people in the Government are troubled today by the things they see in official capacities and they feel helpless because of what happened to Andy Susce. Well, what protection do they have? Not much, really. A civil servant has to take his chances and either he goes to the top and something comes of it, or he gets the Andy Susce treatment."

In another law office, on the opposite side of the city, Attorney Sherman had expressed similar fears for the civil servant. "This country operates because of our decent civil servants. The stability of our nation is on their shoulders. These people obey the laws and they're the heart of this tremendous republic. We rely on them. If we had to rely on the politicians who take all the bows, we'd be a lunatic nation, let me tell you, and we'd have to start over every four years. We mustn't discourage or crush these people. But they're constantly intimidated by politicians. *That* could be our downfall."

Sherman paused, cleaned his black-framed glasses with his handkerchief, and continued. "Andy Susce was a civil servant and he had no avenue of redress. The only redress was political redress and the only way to get that was to have the voters rush to their representatives and urge them to pass a special act recognizing the work done by Susce and the benefits that his report handed to the country. There should be a resolution adopted that Susce be reinstated in his office with full seniority and benefits accorded to him. The least they should do is give him some kind of money settlement. And then the politicians should amend the civil service laws to see that this can*not* happen again."

Back at his home in Newton Falls, Susce pursued Sherman's advice. Once again he wrote his Congressman, Charles J. Carney, requesting the representative to introduce a private bill for him, with the specifications outlined by Attorney Sherman.

In February, 1978, Carney responded.

*"Dear Mr. Susce: . . . As you know, Andrew, I am very sympathetic to your problem . . . With respect to a private relief bill for your back pay, damages and pension, it has been my policy ever since I first became a Member of Congress in November, 1970, not to introduce any private relief bills. For one thing, the House of Representatives has very strict rules regarding the introduction and consideration of such bills.*

*"However, the Senate's rules regarding private relief bills are a little more relaxed; so, if you can get Senator [Howard] Metzenbaum or Senator [John] Glenn to get a private relief bill for you passed in the Senate, I will do everything in my power to get your bill through the House of Representatives as well . . . With kindest regards and best wishes, I am Charles J. Carney, Congressman."*

The letter was disheartening but it didn't altogether dash Susce's hopes. Senator Metzenbaum's aide, Ellen Shifrin, continued to unravel the facts of his case. Susce knew that she was sympathetic to his cause and that she recognized the injustice that had occurred. Shifrin had telephoned Susce on numerous occasions to clarify various points. Susce knew that she had also talked with Attorneys Sherman and Anderson, verifying the information that Susce had sent to her, challenging the tax agency's claim that Susce's investigation was unauthorized. So it seemed to Susce of minor concern that Congressman Carney refused to introduce a bill for him. Senator Metzenbaum would press the Internal Revenue Service for justice and he, Susce thought, would eventually see that justice was done.

"It won't be long now," Susce said to his daughter, Gwendolyn. "Senator Metzenbaum is on his way."

On March 1, 1978, Susce's mailman handed him a letter from Senator Metzenbaum in Washington, D.C. Nervously, Susce tore open the envelope. He sat in the bright, blue love seat that occupied a corner of his enclosed, summer porch, hoping to read the words that he'd been waiting to hear for more than thirty years. Immediately, he recognized the letterhead of the Internal Revenue Service. The letter had been addressed to the Honorable Howard Metzenbaum of Ohio, and it had been signed by Billy J. Brown, the agency's Personnel Director.

"*Dear Senator Metzenbaum,*" Susce read solemnly. "*Your communication to Commissioner Jerome Kurtz regarding one of your constituents, Mr. Andrew Susce, has been referred to me for reply. You enclosed various materials which you had received from Mr. Susce. Mr. Susce is taking issue with the statement in the July 29, 1977, letter to you in which I stated that Mr. Susce made solo fraud investigations which were neither authorized by his superiors nor consistent with existing operating procedures. No information in the materials Mr. Susce forwarded gives reason to cause a reversal of this conclusion. Mr. Susce was removed from the Internal Revenue Service in 1944 on the charge of making allegations against his superior officers, reflecting upon his official integrity, which allegations had no basis in fact. Mr. Susce exhausted his administrative appeals. In the past years, several reviews of the case have been conducted, and in every instance the reviews have sustained the merits of Mr. Susce's removal. Sincerely, Billy J. Brown.*"

Senator Metzenbaum's investigation had met its dead end. The Susce case was closed.

The letter was a paradox. If Susce had been dismissed for "making allegations against his superior officer reflecting upon his official integrity, which allegations had no basis in fact," then why was Brown so concerned about the allegation that Susce had made "solo fraud investigations which were neither authorized by his superiors nor consistent with existing operating procedures"? If Susce, as Brown claimed, had made unauthorized investigations, then it didn't make sense for IRS Collector Stanley Granger, in 1953, to tell the investigating Grand Jury that the Susce Report had been sent to the IRS Intelligence Division for further investigation. Furthermore, if Susce had made unauthorized investigations, then why wasn't he fired for that reason, specifically?

"The IRS knows," Susce told his daughter, whom he had called to listen to Senator Metzenbaum's letter, "that the allegations I made about my superior officers were correct. My report was ditched for ten years! That proves it. They wanted to kill the report. Now the IRS has to come up with a new fix, so they say I didn't have authorization to do the investigation. I had a letter from J. Edgar Hoover—a bureau letter—and that gave me every right under the law of the United States to do what I done. I would have been a crazy man to investigate John Sebastian LaRocca on my own."

Gwendolyn had heard the story time and time before. "All right, Daddy, don't get excited, it's the same thing you've been up against all your life." She worried that her father's distress might cause a stroke.

"And even if I done it on my own, which I didn't," Susce continued, ignoring his daughter's advice, "I showed the government how to collect $180 million of taxes, and I was just scratching the surface. I exposed the Mafia in the United States, not even J. Edgar Hoover knew what I knew, and I wrote one of the most explosive reports ever to hit Washington. And look what they done to me in return." Susce closed his eyes and slid deeper into the soft love seat. He shook his head from side to side and locked his arms across his chest. "If only I had kept a copy of that bureau letter," he said, subdued. "If only I had . . ." he mumbled. And he fell asleep.

The next morning, Susce sat in the front room where the Madonna with outstretched arms was the center of attraction. He felt old. He was tired. It wasn't his seventy-two years that had worn him out, but rather the disappointments. Since 1944, there had been so many. It was as if he had lived a life of perpetual defeat, cognizant of the word victory but never achieving it. Nonetheless, Susce was not a man to pity. He was down, but he'd been down most of his life. He had bucked the system, voluntarily, and he was paying a dreadful price. Given the opportunity, he would do it again, for he never really had a choice. His principles were never flexible.

He knew he could survive a life of disappointments, but never one of shame. His solace was knowing that he had acted honorably. The system had blackened his name, but not his character. And his spirit could not be crushed. He sat now, with a letter pad in his lap and a pen gripped tightly in his fingers. "To the Honorable John Glenn, United States Senator," he wrote. "My name is Andrew J. Susce and I am writing to tell you that the Internal Revenue Service of this great land has persecuted me for more than thirty years . . ."